מסורה

ArtScroll Series®

Rabbi Nosson Scherman / Rabbi Meir Zlotowitz

General Editors

A PROJECT OF THE

Mesorah Heritage Foundation

ל״ג בעומר

Compiled by
Rabbi Shimon Finkelman

Overview by
Rabbi Nosson Scherman

Lag Ba'omer

LAG BA'OMER — ITS OBSERVANCE, LAWS AND SIGNIFICANCE /
A PRESENTATION BASED ON TALMUDIC AND TRADITIONAL SOURCES.

Published by
Mesorah Publications, ltd

FIRST EDITION
First Impression ... April 1999

Published and Distributed by
MESORAH PUBLICATIONS, LTD.
4401 Second Avenue / Brooklyn, N.Y 11232

Distributed in Europe by
J. LEHMANN HEBREW BOOKSELLERS
20 Cambridge Terrace
Gateshead, Tyne and Wear
England NE8 1RP

Distributed in Israel by
SIFRIATI / A. GITLER
10 Hashomer Street
Bnei Brak 51361

Distributed in Australia and New Zealand by
GOLDS BOOK & GIFT SHOP
36 William Street
Balaclava 3183, Vic., Australia

Distributed in South Africa by
KOLLEL BOOKSHOP
Shop 8A Norwood Hypermarket
Norwood 2196, Johannesburg, South Africa

THE ARTSCROLL MESORAH SERIES®
"LAG BA'OMER"/ IT'S OBSERVANCE, LAWS, AND SIGNIFICANCE

ISBN:
1-57819-262-5 (hard cover)
1-57819-263-3 (paperback)

Typography by CompuScribe at ArtScroll Studios, Ltd.

Printed in the United States of America by Noble Book Press Corp.
Bound by Sefercraft, Quality Bookbinders, Ltd., Brooklyn N.Y. 11232

This volume is dedicated by:

Sendy and Kranie Liebhard

In Honor of our Parents

Pinchus and Agi Liebhard

Sholom and Eva Stern

and our children

Aryeh, Elisha, Nechama,

Rachelli and Malky

❖ ❖ ❖

Vivian and Stanley Bernstein

In Honor of our Parents

Adele and Jules Bernstein

Renee and Andrew Weiss

and our children

Michelle, Jamie, Jesse and Nicole

❖ ❖ ❖

Melly and Rochelle Lifshitz

In Honor of our Parents

Daniel and Claire Lifshitz

Benjamin and Lillian Rottenstein

and our children

J.D., Adam, Arye, Aliza and Ariella

מכתב ברכה מאת הרב ר' משה וואלפסאן שליט"א
משגיח רוחני דמתיבתא תורה ודעת
ורב דבהמ"ד אמונת ישראל

בע"ה

הרב משה וואלפסאן
RABBI MOSHE WOLFSON
1619 - 41st STREET
BROOKLYN, NEW YORK
11218

ב"ה ו' ניסן תשנ"ט

אל ידידי האהוב, מזכה הרבים, הרה"ג ר' שמעון פינקלמאן שליט"א.

ברוך אתה וברוך טעמך שבחרת לך התפקיד הקדוש והנכבד לכתוב ספרים לדוברי אנגלית המדוברת במדינתנו. ספרים כאלה בעניני מוסר, תולדות צדיקים, וחיבורים המאירים את תוכן החגים, הם מים קרים על נפש עיפה של הנוער (וגם המבוגרים) הצמאים לחיים של תוכן, המבקשים לשמוע את דבר ד' האמת; והבוחלים באומר הקריאה של רוח הזמן המציפים את אמתה של תורה והמבטלים את כל העת בספרי השגב נכריה. חוננך השי"ת בלשון למודים באמר עליון, וכשרונות נעלים, והקוראים בספריך נמשכים אחרי דבריך הפועלים בלבם הטוי לטובה, ללכת בדרכי ישרים ולהטות לבבם לתורת השי"ת ועבודתו.

בודאי זה תפקידך בעולם, ולשליחות מיוחדת זו נשלחת לעולם. וכבר זכית שנעשו דבריך בלבות אלפים ורבבות מבני עמנו. לך בכחך זה והושעת את ישראל.

אשרי חלקך שעלה בידך לכתוב חיבור המפיץ אורה על פרשת גבורת התנא האלקי רשב"י, ספרו הזוהר, וחג ל"ג בעומר. התנא הזה וספרו הנפלא כולו עטוף מסתורין, והעיד בדקותו, מי יבוא ויבוא באיצה מידה, את שרשת החמדה ויגלה את מכסה העתיק, ע"כ לידע מי הוא זה ומה רב טובו. בטוח אני בעזה"י שיתקבל חיבורך בחיבה יתירה אצל בני עמנו, ויהי' לתועלת ולטובה לנפש תדרשנו.

בברכת ידידות,
משה וואלפסאן

⇝ Publisher's Preface

As the ArtScroll Holiday Series comes to its conclusion, with this eleventh book in the series, we look back at books that are serving the community very well. This combination of ideas, history, laws, insights, and prayers has been instructive and inspiring to many thousands of people. For this we are indebted to the authors who contributed to the series. Their scholarship, *yiras Shamayim,* and dedication to the needs of the *klal* have earned them the respect and gratitude of multitudes; we are proud of our association with them.

To most Jews, especially outside of Israel, Lag B'Omer is a day for school trips, weddings, and haircuts, but it is much more. It is an amalgam of significant themes: the original Sefirah days leading up to the giving of the Torah at Mount Sinai, the agricultural festivities in Eretz Yisrael, the tragedy of Rabbi Akiva's students and the stirring saga of Rabbi Shimon bar Yochai invest Lag B'Omer with much history and meaning. In this book, the reader will become familiar with all these facets of Lag B'Omer and develop a new appreciation for the importance of the day and what it represents.

We are grateful to **Sendy Liebhard,** one of the dedicators of this book, who suggested that this project be undertaken and who offered valuable suggestions about its contents. We look forward to his continued friendship, together with his associates **Stanley Bernstein** and **Melly Lifshitz.**

Rabbi Shimon Finkelman, a familiar author to ArtScroll readers, has produced a book that will be enlightening even to scholars. Always an assiduous researcher, he went to special pains in preparing this manuscript, and it shows in the final product. We are grateful, as many thousands of readers will be.

Rabbi Meir Zlotowitz / Rabbi Nosson Scherman
Nissan 5759 / March 1999

✥ Acknowledgements

This work is drawn from a wide range of sources. While it would be quite difficult to list them all, a few must be mentioned.

Extensive use has been made of the works of the noted Kabbalist, R' Yeshaya Asher Zelig Margulies, especially *Hilula D'Rashbi* and *Midos Rashbi.*

A number of Hebrew anthologies on Lag BaOmer have been useful, particularly *Chagim U'Zemanim — Lag BaOmer* and *Gal Peninim.* Mention must be made of the historical work *Toldos Am Olam* by Rabbi Shlomo Rottenberg, which contains a detailed chapter on the life of R' Shimon bar Yochai and the development of his *Sefer HaZohar.*

Other works of note are mentioned in the preface to "Selected Laws and Customs."

I am deeply grateful to Rabbi Meir Zlotowitz for inviting me to undertake this project and to Rabbi Nosson Scherman for always being available to offer guidance and assistance. As always, Rabbi Scherman's Overview lends a beautiful, unique dimension to the book.

The graphics master Reb Sheah Brander has produced a work of true graphic beauty. The striking cover is the work of Reb Eli Kroen and Danny Kaye. As always, Avrohom Biderman has served as an able and patient project coordinator and sounding board. My thanks also to Rabbi Yaakov Hersh Horowitz, Shaya Sonnenschein and Chumie Zaidman for their skillful typing and paginating; to Mrs. Faigie Weinbaum for her meticulous proofreading; and to the entire staff at ArtScroll/Mesorah.

I am grateful for the opportunity to express my *hakaras hatov* to my *rebbi,* HaRav Moshe Wolfson, שליט"א, who gave of his precious time to clarify many points related to this volume. As the reader will note, many of HaRav Wolfson's thoughts, as recorded in *Emunas*

Itecha, are found in this work. May Hashem grant him many years of good health to teach, guide and inspire.

My eternal gratitude to my parents, שיחיו, for all that they have done for me, as well as to my in-laws, שיחיו, to whom I owe so much. I recognize and appreciate that my work would not be possible were it not for the support and encouragement of my wife, Tova, תחי׳.

I thank the *Ribono shel Olam* for permitting me to undertake and complete this project. May the day of Lag BaOmer bring a flow of blessing and salvation to each Jew individually and to our nation as a whole.

Shimon Finkelman

Nissan 5759

Table of Contents

An Overview / Rabbi Shimon bar Yochai and the Omer

⁂ An Overview / Rabbi Shimon bar Yochai and the Omer

I. Return to Awareness

Ten Utterances

God created the world with Ten Utterances; then it became the task of man to perceive the Divine Presence in every facet of the universe.

God created the world with ten utterances (*Avos* 5:1); then it became the task of man to perceive the Divine Presence in every facet of the universe. He could look at the sun and say that God created it on the fourth day and made it earth's source of light and energy; look at the land around him and say that God swept away the oceans on the fifth day and revealed the continents, look at the vastness of space through the Hubble telescope and say that it testifies more than previous generations even imagined to the infinite scope and power of God's Creation. Man could look in the mirror and say that God created him on the sixth day and put him in charge of the world, with the responsibility to guide it and himself according to the Heavenly will.

Or man could erroneously see himself and say how marvelous that a few cells could split randomly, mutate and evolve through countless millennia and become an organism with intelligence, the power of speech and ability to rule the world.

There is another alternative, just as corrosive, one that infiltrated humanity during the 10 generations from Adam to Noah, and again after Noah. Man could acknowledge that God, only God, created everything, but then He placed them under the control of heavenly bodies and forces of nature, and they, as God's agents, were deserving of tribute, just as one honors the ministers of government. This in itself is idolatry, but it grew worse. Eventually, man would forget that these forces were merely agents and remember only that they are to be worshiped, and come to think that they were independent deities. Of such flights of imagination spiced with logic was idolatry born.

Of such flights of imagination spiced with logic was idolatry born.

And so humanity fell from Adam's spiritual precipice until its awareness of the Ten Utterances became obscured and forgotten entirely. In Egypt, the Nile was god. The sheep was god. Pharaoh was god. So degraded had man become that when Moses and Aaron came with God's command to Pharaoh that he allow the Children of Israel to serve God in the Wilderness, the king bellowed, as much in ignorance as defiance, *"Who is* HASHEM *that I should heed His voice to send out Israel!"* (*Exodus* 5:2).

If the Ten Utterances were forgotten, then the One Who uttered them was forgotten as well.

If the Ten Utterances were forgotten, then the One Who uttered them was forgotten as well. As Scripture states throughout the miracles of the Exodus, the Ten Plagues were intended to demonstrate to everyone — to Pharaoh, his people, and even to the Jews, who had languished so long in the hotbed of idolatry and sorcery — that Hashem was God, the only God, and that neither His heavenly handmaidens nor His earthly forces were acceptable subjects of worship. This point is apparent from the Ten Commandments, which begin, *"I am* HASHEM, *your God, Who has taken you out of the land of Egypt, from the house of slavery"* (*Exodus* 20:2), as if to say that — in contrast to Pharaoh, who denied knowledge of Hashem — the Exodus proves that only He is God.

Strip Away Barriers

AS EXPLAINED BY *CHIDDUSHEI HARIM*, THE TEN PLAGUES were meant to strip away the barriers concealing the reality of the Ten Utterances. Life on earth is a constant exercise of cause and effect, and it takes an honest intellectual effort to see His hand in events and His creativity in existence. Seen superficially, how could anyone deny that Pharaoh or a current superpower or science controls history? One can *see* the political, military and economic power, but God's power is invisible, just as He is invisible. Each plague shattered a delusion that prevented people from "hearing" a creative utterance of God, until the tenth plague restored faith in the First Cause, the Creator.

Each plague shattered a delusion that prevented people from "hearing" a creative utterance of God.

When the Ten Plagues were done, Israel, if not other nations, returned to the pristine awareness that Creation began with God, and that it continues only because of His constant life-giving force. As we say in the daily *Shacharis* liturgy, וּבְטוּבוֹ מְחַדֵּשׁ בְּכָל יוֹם תָּמִיד מַעֲשֵׂה בְרֵאשִׁית, *in His goodness, [God] renews daily, perpetually, the work of creation.*

To illustrate this concept, the ninth plague was darkness, a darkness so thick and intense that it was palpable and the Egyptians could not move — but during that darkness, the Jews had light in their dwelling places (*Exodus* 21-23). Aside from the literal meaning of the passage, *Chiddushei HaRim* explains that the darkness that enveloped Egypt strengthened the faith and perception of the Jews to the point where they recognized in the universe the continuing existence of the second utterance of creation, יְהִי אוֹר, *Let there be light* (*Genesis 1:3*). The darkness that descended upon Egypt revealed the light of truth.

The darkness that descended upon Egypt revealed the light of truth.

The Origin of All

THE TENTH PLAGUE WAS THE DEATH OF THE FIRSTBORN, which had a profound symbolism, in addition to the profound grief and destruction it brought upon Egypt. The firstborn represents a new beginning of generation, a new stage in the life of a family. The first utterance of Creation was בְּרֵאשִׁית, *In the beginning* (*Genesis* 1:1*;* see *Rosh Hashanah* 32a). Although that word was not a command that something come into being, it was, in a sense, the greatest of all the utterances, because it taught the concept that in the beginning, before anything else existed, there was God, the only Being with the power to create *ex nihilo*. When the firstborn, the human embodiment of hope for the future, was destroyed, it brought a new awareness that all beginnings are the province of God alone, that if He wills it, people, continents and planets are created; if not, there is only astonishing emptiness.

If He wills it, people, continents and planets are created; if not, there is only astonishing emptiness.

II. The Omer Count

To Climb the Mountain

Those who experienced the miracles were elevated to a very high level of spiritual perception.

THE MIRACLES OF THE EXODUS DEMONSTRATED these truths to the Jewish people beyond any doubt. Those who experienced the miracles were elevated to a very high level of spiritual perception, so much so that at the Splitting of the Sea, the simplest person attained a degree of prophecy even above that of the prophet Ezekiel. But that was an unearned gift. That degree of spiritual greatness was lost as soon as it was no longer needed; the nation of slaves could not automatically remain a nation of prophets. From then on, the people had to elevate themselves through their own efforts.

Having enjoyed the temporary gift of greatness, their desire to be worthy of it had been kindled. It was like someone who was taken on a helicopter to the top of a mountain and enjoyed the bracing air, the challenging slope and the breath taking view. Then the helicopter brought him back down and he was told, "You can have the experience whenever you want it, but only if you learn to climb on your own." Could he do it? No, not yet. But if he worked day by day to condition himself and learned how to scale peaks, he could *earn* his way to the top.

If he worked day by day to condition himself and learned how to scale peaks, he could earn his way to the top.

So it was with Israel as they left Egypt. They had tasted spiritual greatness. Could they taste it again? Could a nation whose spirituality had been ground down by generations of exposure to the degeneracy of

Egypt and then by more than a century of brutal slavery ever become a kingdom of priests and a holy nation? Moses himself doubted it, but God had assured him, *"When you take the people out of Egypt, you will serve God on this mountain* [Sinai]" (*Exodus* 3:12; see *Rashi*).

With the Exodus, the effort began. In seven weeks they would stand around Mount Sinai.

With the Exodus, the effort began. In seven weeks they would stand around Mount Sinai, ready to receive the Ten Commandments. Would they be ready?

The day after they left Egypt, they began counting the forty-nine days of preparation, every day rising higher, until they reached the summit that God had promised Moses.

Up from Forty-nine Gates

AS THE SAGES TEACH, THE EGYPT ORDEAL HAD CAST THE Jews down to the forty-ninth degree of spiritual contamination [מ״ט שערי טומאה]. Just a bit more and they would have fallen to the fiftieth and lowest level, the depth from which it would have been impossible to extricate themselves. Beginning with the second day of Pesach — the day after they left Egyptian domination — they counted each passing day in anticipation of the rendezvous at Sinai. Day by day they rose from a level of contamination to the corresponding degree of holiness, and after forty-nine days of effort, they had lifted themselves to the forty-ninth degree of holiness. Once again they were ready for the prophecy at Sinai. This time, however, it was not an unearned gift, but a deserved prize.

Day by day they rose from a level of contamination to the corresponding degree of holiness.

In the words of Rabbi Moshe Chaim Luzzatto (*Maamar HaChochmah, Sefiras HaOmer*):

> The matter of *Sefiras HaOmer* [i.e., the Counting of the Omer, the forty-nine days from Pesach to Shavuos, see below] is as follows: Fifty gates of understanding were created in the world, and Moses degree of comprehension included forty-nine gates, but he could not comprehend the fiftieth gate,

which is the ultimate [level] of understanding. Those [forty-nine levels are the] forty-nine days of the Counting of the Omer, and the Torah was given on the fiftieth day.

God makes influences for good and evil to balance one another, so that man will have the challenge of exercising his free will.

Just as there are forty-nine gates of understanding and holiness, so there are forty-nine gates of [spiritual] contamination, for *God has made one corresponding to the other* (*Koheles* 7:14) [i.e. God makes influences for good and evil to balance one another, so that man will have the challenge of exercising his free will] — the Good Inclination and the Evil Inclination, the one with its purity and the other with its contamination, in conflicting aspects.

When Israel was in Egypt, they were sunk and soiled in forty-nine gates of contamination, and they had to escape from them. God wished to extricate Israel from them and to subjugate those forty-nine gates of contamination. But He did so step by step, by illuminating a gate of holiness opposite its corresponding gate of contamination, one on each of the days from after the first day of Pesach until Shavuos.

This perfection is aroused anew every year by means of counting the forty-nine days of the Omer.

This perfection is aroused anew every year by means of counting the forty-nine days of the Omer between Pesach, the day of the liberation, until Shavuos, the day the Torah is given, which is the illumination of the fiftieth gate of understanding and holiness upon Israel.

Omer — the Link

THE TORAH BINDS PESACH TO SHAVUOS THROUGH THE Counting of the Omer. Indeed, the Shavuos festival is not even given a calendar date in the Torah; it is described only as the fiftieth day, the day after the forty-nine days of counting, which implies clearly that the giving of the Torah was conditioned on Israel's readiness for it, as acquired during the seven weeks of preparation.

The days of Sefiras HaOmer link Pesach and Shavuos, and demonstrate their unity of purpose.

Ramban and others have described the days between Pesach and Shavuos in terms of the Intermediate Days of festivals. Just as Pesach and Succos have Intermediate Days that connect the first and last days of those festivals, so the days of *Sefiras HaOmer* link Pesach and Shavuos, and demonstrate their unity of purpose. This connection between the two festivals is especially so since Shavuos is the "fiftieth day," just as the last day of Pesach is called the seventh day of the festival. The above discussion makes clear why this is so. Freedom must have a purpose, otherwise it is anarchy. As God told Moses, Israel was being freed from Egypt in order that it would be able to receive the Torah at Sinai. Going further back in history, this would be the fulfillment of the mission of Abraham, Isaac and Jacob. Without the Torah, there was no reason for the Exodus, and the Jewish slaves would not only have remained in Egypt, but eventually would have become submerged into the Egyptian nation and would have disappeared as a separate nationality, as has happened to so many other peoples throughout history.

Without the Torah, there was no reason for the Exodus.

The degree of one's infusion with the holiness of Shavuos depends on the degree of one's success during the preparation period.

There had to be a progression from Pesach to Shavuos, and the Omer days inculcated into Israel then and always an awareness that we must use these seven weeks as a time of striving and growth. Given this principle, it is reasonable that the degree of one's infusion with the holiness of Shavuos depends on the degree of one's success during the preparation period of the Omer days. If the Jewish people in the Wilderness had not climbed the spiritual ladder leading up to Sinai, they would not have reached its summit.

Common Denominator

CHIDDUSHEI HARIM AND *SFAS EMES* MAKE THIS POINT by referring to the Talmudic principle of *Klal U'frat U'chlal*: כְּלָל וּפְרָט וּכְלָל, אִי אַתָּה דָן אֶלָּא כְּעֵין הַפְּרָט, *if a general statement is followed by a specification, followed in turn by another general statement — you may infer only whatever is similar to the specification.* For example, in the verse imposing a fine on a thief, there are two general terms — *for every item of liability* and *for any lost item* — implying that the thief is liable no matter what sort of item he has stolen. However, sandwiched between these two general terms is mention of a number of specific items: *an ox, a donkey, a sheep, or a garment (Exodus* 22:8). This teaches that the fine applies only to items that are similar to the enumerated ones. Just as they are all movable objects that have intrinsic value, so too the fine applies only to similar items, but not to real estate, which is not movable, or to IOU's, which testify to the existence of a debt, but have no monetary value, in and of themselves (*Bava Metzia* 57b).

The days of *Sefiras HaOmer* can be seen in terms of the above hermeneutical principle. Pesach is a national festival. Shavuos is a national festival. The Omer days, on the other hand, are not counted by the Sanhedrin or any other national body. The Talmud applies the commandment of counting to each individual Jew, implying that everyone has the personal responsibility to prepare himself for the giving of the law. And just as *Klal U'frat U'chlal* instructs us that the generality must be interpreted as similar to the specification, so too the spiritual efficacy of Pesach and Shavuos depends on how well the nation's individual components did their job of preparing themselves. Someone who elevated himself to the limit of his ability during the seven weeks will reap a huge spiritual harvest on Shavuos. Someone who spent the balmy springtime days of *Sefirah* enjoying the weather and planning his summer vacation will barely notice the spiritual potential of Shavuos, just as he will fail to gain the true freedom offered by Pesach.

Someone who elevated himself to the limit of his ability during the seven weeks will reap a huge spiritual harvest on Shavuos.

From Barley to Wheat

THIS CONCEPT IS ALLUDED TO IN THE CONTENTS OF THE offerings of the Omer and Shavuos. The Omer offering consists of barley flour from the new crop. The Two Loaves of the Shavuos *mussaf* offering are made with wheat flour of the new crop (see *Rambam, Hil. Temidim u'Mussafim*). The Sages speak of barley as an inferior food, a food which is customarily used for animals rather than human beings. Wheat, on the other hand, is described as the quintessential human food, and is even used homiletically to symbolize human intelligence. Thus, the seven-week Omer period begins with animal food and ends with human food, symbolizing Israel's need during this period to grow and advance, from inferiority to excellence, from physical freedom to the ultimate freedom of the rule of the intellect over the senses, from the law of Pharaoh to the law of God.

The seven-week Omer period begins with animal food and ends with human food.

Sh'lah HaKadosh teaches that the temporal world is a metaphor for the spiritual world, which is the ultimate world of truth. The sun is a metaphor for the Torah, which is the true light. Eyes are a metaphor for God, the all-seeing "Eye," which sees all and knows all. Life-giving rain and dew are metaphors for God's power over life. So, too, the pleasant weather of the season of *Sefiras HaOmer*, which nurtures the crops as they ripen, is a metaphor for the spiritual "weather" of the days leading up to the giving of the Torah in ancient times, and Israel's annual rendezvous with the gift of Torah.

Sabbath-weeks

THE WAY IN WHICH THE TORAH EXPRESSES THE COMmandment to count indicates this need to grow:

וּסְפַרְתֶּם לָכֶם . . . שֶׁבַע שַׁבָּתוֹת תְּמִימֹת תִּהְיֶינָה

You shall count for yourselves . . . seven Sabbaths (*Leviticus* 23:15).

Rather than referring to the weeks of counting by the more common term שָׁבֻעוֹת, as it does in *Deuteronomy* 16:9, the Torah refers to the weeks as Sabbaths, indicating that the nature of the week being counted should be seen in the relationship of the six weekdays to the Sabbath. An ordinary week is nothing more than a total of seven days, none more significant than any of the others. A *Sabbath-week* is defined as a period in which

A Sabbath-week is defined as a period in which the six weekdays are molded and nourished by the Sabbath.

the six weekdays are molded and nourished by the Sabbath. The Sabbath is the calendar's source of holiness. It is the day that God *blessed and sanctified*, the day that is a *heritage, a remembrance of Creation* (*Friday Night Kiddush*).

In this sense, the Sabbath is the primary day of the week, because it infuses holiness into the other six days. The Sages comment that a circumcision is performed on the eighth day so that the infant will live through a holy Sabbath before entering the covenant. But if so, why shouldn't the circumcision be performed on the first Sunday of the baby's life, as soon as the first Sabbath is over? The answer is that what is needed is not only the twenty-four hours of the Sabbath, but a full week that has absorbed the sanctity of the Sabbath.

Just as the Sabbath elevates its neighboring days, so he must let himself and his aspirations be elevated. The Sages

So, too, the weeks of *Sefirah* must be *Sabbath-weeks*, not merely groups of seven days. As a Jew counts his forty-nine days of accomplishment, he must recognize that just as the Sabbath elevates its neighboring days, so he must let himself and his aspirations be elevated as he mounts the rungs toward the summit of his personal Mount Sinai. The Jewish people emerged from the Egyptian exile with two gifts, freedom and Torah. As the soul of the week, the Sabbath teaches that freedom must be inseparable from the Torah, otherwise it loses its meaning.

Roots of Festivals

Let no one think that Pesach, *Sefirah*, and Shavuos are merely anniversaries of historic events. Very few of the myriad miracles and significant events of Jewish history are part of the religious calendar; only the Scriptural festivals and the Rabbinic holidays of Purim and Chanukah are observed every year. Jewish tradition teaches that the spiritual emanations of the select festivals are repeated every year. Emanations of holiness reach the world on the Sabbath, of forgiveness on Yom Kippur, of freedom on Pesach, of Torah on Shavuos. Legislatures may manipulate the dates of secular holidays in order to create long weekends that will maximize leisure time and minimize disruption of business, but the Heavenly festival cycle is unchanging and unchangeable.

recognized that spiritual reverberations of Chanukah and Purim would come back year after year.

One might wonder why the Sages chose to make a festival to commemorate the miracle of Chanukah, for example, and not Joshua's miracle of stopping the sun (*Joshua* 10:12), or that of Elijah on Mount Carmel (*I Kings* 18:35-39). The answer is that the Sages, with their Divinely guided wisdom, recognized that spiritual reverberations of Chanukah — and Purim, as well — would come back year after year. In recognition of this, the Sages ordained that we recite the blessing שֶׁעָשָׂה נִסִּים לַאֲבוֹתֵינוּ בַּיָּמִים הָהֵם בַּזְּמַן הַזֶּה, *Who wrought miracles for our forefathers, in those days at this season*, meaning that though the miracles actually occurred in ancient times *in those days*, their influence is still with us *at this season* (*Kedushas Levi*). Such a blessing is not needed for the Scripturally ordained festivals, because the Torah testifies to their ongoing sanctity.

This potential for renewed sanctity is why the commentators attach such significance to the days of *Sefirah*. From the start, this was a time of unstinting effort to rise to great heights. So it must remain in our time.

III. The Students of Rabbi Akiva

Dramatic Punishment

To comprehend the enormity of the tragedy, one must remember the history of that era.

HISTORICALLY, THE TIME OF *SEFIRAS HAOMER* WAS A time of rejoicing. Materially, it was the time when the crops were maturing and ripening. Spiritually, too, Jews were maturing and ripening, from the freedom of Pesach to the Torah of Shavuos. Then, these days were plunged into mourning, as the 24,000 students of Rabbi Akiva died during this period. To comprehend the enormity of the tragedy, one must remember the history of that era. The Roman Empire had destroyed the Second Temple and held the remnants of the nation in a cruel and iron grip. Rabbi Akiva was the greatest sage of his time, the pillar of the Oral Law, whose teaching was keeping the Torah alive among the Jewish people. It should be recalled that in his later years, the Romans forbade the teaching of the Oral Law, and Rabbi Akiva was tortured to death for defying their decree. The loss of his students, therefore, quite apart from their great number, was a calamity of historic proportions, virtually denuding the Jewish people of hope for its spiritual future.

The loss of his students, therefore, quite apart from their great number, was a calamity of historic proportions. Rabbi Akiva was

The sin of the disciples, the Talmud teaches, was that they did not show sufficient honor to one another (*Yevamos* 62b). After the tragedy, mindful of what had happened before, Rabbi Akiva admonished his new students, "My sons, the earlier ones died because they begrudged one another. Be diligent not to do as they did." The new students — there were only five — stood fast and filled the entire world with Torah (*Bereishis Rabbah* 61:3).

Why was that sin punished so dramatically? Surely their shortcoming existed for a long time — why did the punishment come just during the days of *Sefiras HaOmer?*

To Be United

AT THE OUTSET, IT SHOULD BE CLEAR THAT GREAT MEN are judged by strict standards, and Rabbi Akiva's students were surely great. Their failure to show proper respect for one another was not in the least comparable to the sort of friction and acrimony that permeates many a contemporary academic precinct, but whatever there was should not have existed among such scholars and in the study hall of such a Torah giant.

the epitome of loving unity among Jews.

Rabbi Akiva was the epitome of loving unity among Jews. It was he who said, "Love your fellow as yourself, that is the main principle of the Torah; the rest is commentary" (*Toras Kohanim* 11:12). In the slightly different formulation of Hillel the Elder, of whose academy Rabbi Akiva was a student, "What is hateful to you, do not do to your comrade. This is the entire Torah; the rest is commentary" (*Shabbos* 31a). Certainly it is important to love one's fellow, but how can that commandment include all the other six-hundred-twelve commandments to the degree that one can say the rest is but commentary?

Someone too selfish to care about others will not subjugate himself to God either.

The *Chazon Ish* commented that someone too selfish to care about others will not subjugate himself to God either; his own desires and ego will always get in the way. What Hillel and Rabbi Akiva meant was that unselfish love of others is the character trait that is a precondition for service of God. With it, one can accept the yoke of all the commandments; without it, the yoke will always manage to slip off his shoulders whenever it becomes inconvenient.

It is instructive that in giving the numbers of Rabbi Akiva's students, the Talmud does not say there were 24,000. It says he had *12,000 pairs* of students. The obvious connotation is that Talmudic study is most successful with a partner, so that, through the natural process of debate and challenge, the partners can refine their arguments and arrive at the truth. There is an additional connotation. Rabbi Akiva, the exemplar of love for others, wanted his students to think of themselves as partners, rather than as individuals.

Rabbi Akiva, the exemplar of love for others, wanted his students to think of themselves as partners, rather than as individuals.

This attitude was necessary in order for the Jewish people to acquire the Torah. In stating that Israel encamped at Mount Sinai, the Torah emphasizes that they were unified: וַיִּחַן שָׁם יִשְׂרָאֵל נֶגֶד הָהָר, *and Israel* [in the singular] *encamped there opposite the mountain (Exodus* 19:2). Quoting the *Mechilta, Rashi* comments: "[they encamped] as one man, with one heart, but all the other encampments were with complaints and argumentation."

Striking a Balance

THE DAYS OF *SEFIRAH*, AS NOTED ABOVE, ARE A TIME when people are charged to strive for improvement as *individuals*, but at the same time they must strive for

The crescendo of argumentation in a crowded study hall is a good example.

unity. The crescendo of argumentation in a crowded study hall is a good example of how these two seemingly contradictory impulses can be combined. The Talmud interprets the phrase אוֹיְבִים בַּשָּׁעַר, *enemies in the gate* (*Psalms* 127:5), as referring to people studying Torah together. "Even a father and a son or a teacher and his student who are studying Torah together in one gate, [at first] become enemies of one another, but they do not move from there until they become devoted friends of one another" (*Kiddushin* 30b).

The enmity was not real; the love was.

When people are searching for the truth, they will dispute one another strenuously, but when they arrive at a correct conclusion, they will embrace and kiss — figuratively, if not literally — the intellectual opponents who helped them find it. The enmity was not real; the love was.

Such would have been the ideal state of Rabbi Akiva's study hall: fierce argumentation leading to the truth and the shared joy and love that flows from it. This requires a balance between the striving of the individual and his responsibility to the community. The balance was lacking. His students waged the battle for personal growth, but they begrudged one another proper credit for their accomplishments, and that led them not to honor one another as they should have.

The Torah demands that one should not begrudge maximum benefits to others.

In discussing how it is humanly possible to love someone else as one loves oneself — and it *must* be possible for ordinary people or the Torah could not have commanded it — *Ramban* explains that indeed one's love for oneself and one's children is greater than one's love for others. That is an undeniable fact. What the Torah demands, however, is that one should not begrudge maximum benefits to others. One should be willing and even happy for others to be wise, righteous, wealthy, accomplished, happy, successful and blessed in any other possible way.

It is not unreasonable for the Torah to demand that one not be jealous of success that is not a threat to anyone. It was there that Rabbi Akiva's students fell short. Such conduct is especially grievous during the days of *Sefirah*, the days when Jews historically strove for self-improvement while strengthening the bonds of unity and fellowship.

Such conduct is especially grievous during the days of Sefirah.

Rambam teaches that a sin during the Ten Days of Repentance, between Rosh Hashanah and Yom Kippur, is worse than a sin at any other time, because those are the days when God longs for our repentance so that He can forgive our sins. At such a time, indifference to sin is especially intolerable. In this sense, the failure of Rabbi Akiva's students was much more glaring than it was during the rest of the year. The days of *Sefirah* are a time to combine individual growth with concern for others (see below), which is why their punishment came just during *Sefirah*.

IV. Rabbi Shimon bar Yochai

Lessons of the Manna

THE SAGES TEACH לֹא נִתְּנָה תּוֹרָה אֶלָּא לְאוֹכְלֵי הַמָּן, *the Torah could be given only to those who ate the manna* (*Mechilta Beshalach* 17). The commentators explain that those who ate the manna in the Wilderness learned that they were entirely dependent on God's kindness. The manna fell every morning and disappeared by midday. None could be saved from day to day. Someone who had no faith that there would be more manna in the morning would have become so consumed with anxiety that he would have been unable to sleep — what would he and his family eat the next day? To live with such fear for forty years would have driven people mad.

There was no anxiety, no fear, because the people had absolute faith that God would provide for them the next day.

But there was no anxiety, no fear, because the people had absolute faith that God would provide for them the next day and the day after that and every day. Such people could accept the Torah with complete trust in the justice of its Giver, and God would give the Torah only to people who were ready to make material concerns secondary to their desire to serve God. So it was that barely two weeks after the manna began to fall, the entire nation would declare to Moses, "Whatever HASHEM says, נַעֲשֶׂה וְנִשְׁמַע, *we will do and we will hear.*"

Rabbi Shimon bar Yochai and Rabbi Eliezer were like their ancestors who lived with total faith.

As the Talmud (*Shabbos* 33b) relates, when Rabbi Shimon bar Yochai and his son Rabbi Eliezer went into hiding from the Romans, they lived in a cave for twelve years, nourished only by a well and a carob tree that God provided for them. They were like their ancestors who lived with total faith that God would provide manna at its assigned time. Just as such faith was a prerequisite for the receiving of the Torah, so it became the source of merit that enabled Rabbi Shimon to receive the hidden wisdom that he inscribed in the Holy *Zohar*, the basic textbook of Kabbalistic knowledge (*Ohr Gedaliahu*).

The Omer's Lesson

THE *OMER* OFFERING, TOO, WAS SYMBOLIC OF SUCH FAITH. It demonstrated that the Jewish people consecrated their first produce to God. The offering itself was rather small, only the volume of 43.2 eggs of fine barley flour, but it was forbidden to use any of the new grain crops before the Omer was offered, as if to say, "O God, You have given us our food for the next year. It is Yours, and we use it only because You permit us to have it."

The manna began to fall on Lag B'Omer, which became the day when Israel rose to a new level of faith.

According to the calculation of *Chasam Sofer*, the manna began to fall on Lag BaOmer, which became the day when Israel rose to a new level of faith in God's providence. It is fitting, therefore, that it was on Lag BaOmer, during the Counting of the Omer, that Rabbi Shimon revealed to his students previously unimagined mysteries of the Torah, and that the sun remained in the sky until he was finished. The day when his sun set was also the day of a momentous sunrise, whose rays still shine brightly, and is still celebrated by a grateful nation. Although the death of a teacher is ordinarily an occasion of great sadness and fasting, Rabbi Shimon instructed his disciples to rejoice, because they had been granted so much knowledge on that great, long day. We are all his disciples, so, in addition to the happiness because Rabbi Akiva's students did not die on Lag BaOmer, we all celebrate Rabbi Shimon Bar Yochai's gift of wisdom, as he requested.

Haman said, "Your handful of flour will overcome my ten thousand silver talents."

The Talmud (*Megillah* 16a) teaches that when Haman, convinced he was about to do away with the hated Mordechai and then the entire Jewish nation, came upon Mordechai and the elders, Haman asked what they were discussing. Mordechai explained that they were reviewing the laws of the Omer offering. Upon hearing what the Omer was, Haman said, "Your handful of flour will overcome my ten thousand silver talents [that Haman had offered for the right to carry out his genocide]."

Strange. Haman had offered an enormous fortune for the right to exterminate the Jewish people; how could a handful of flour outweigh his 10,000 talents of silver?

If the world is cast under the laws of nature, what room is there for hope? But there are miracles hidden inside nature.

Michtav Me'Eliyahu explains what Haman saw in the Omer that so frightened him. In the time of Mordechai and Esther, there were no open miracles, as there had been in previous centuries. If the world is cast under the laws of nature, what room is there for hope against the powerful Hamans and their designs? But there *are* miracles hidden inside nature. The Sages compare the produce of the fields to other human activity. How much work is needed to prepare a cut of meat for human consumption? Yet God provides wind, rain and sun to let the crops grow and provide people with grain (*Yalkut, Esther* 643)!

Elaborating on the *Yalkut, Maharal* writes,

> At a time when there were no [open] miracles and wonders in the world, but the world functioned in its natural manner ... the commandment of the Omer stood up for the Jewish people. They brought the Omer to

the Holy One, Blessed is He, because He guides nature. Nature does not function independently; rather, He controls nature. This is why there is no sacred Name of God in *Megillas Esther*, because in the "natural" course of events [of the Megillah] one does not see His Great Name, which initiates miracles; only by allusion is God mentioned (*Ohr Chadash;* see Overview to ArtScroll *Megillas Esther*).

This is the message of the Omer, that God is in the field no less than in the Temple.

When Haman realized that Jews have faith that God's omnipotence extends to ordinary, everyday events, he feared that his elaborate and expensive plan could yet be dashed — as it was by a series of "coincidences" that were orchestrated by a hidden hand. This is the message of the Omer, that God is in the field no less than in the Temple. Haman was right. It is remarkable that he was hanged on the 16th day of Nissan, the day when the Omer would be offered. Truly, the Omer had a message in time of exile, a time when God is no less present, though He is hidden.

Rabbi Akiva's Response

That Rabbi Akiva, at an advanced age, assembled students again is an extraordinary tribute to his own faith and greatness.

RABBI SHIMON BAR YOCHAI AND HIS COLLEAGUES WERE Rabbi Akiva's response to the loss of his generation of students. After their death, Rabbi Akiva traveled to the south of Eretz Yisrael and began again with Rabbi Shimon, Rabbi Meir, Rabbi Yehudah, Rabbi Elazar and Rabbi Yose (*Yevamos* 62b). That Rabbi Akiva, at an advanced age when his life's work lay in shambles, and in defiance of the Roman prohibition against teaching Torah, assembled students again is an extraordinary tribute to his own faith and greatness. God had taken away his 24,000 students, and undoubtedly many of his peers were plunged into despair, but Rabbi Akiva would not permit the Torah to be forgotten. Virtually the entire Oral Law as we have it was transmitted by those five new disciples of Rabbi Akiva, and we stand in awe at the perse-

His feat should remain an eternal inspiration to all Jews who live through difficult times.

verance of this great and brave sage. His feat should remain an eternal inspiration to all Jews who live through difficult times.

V. Rabbi Shimon's Uniqueness

Sensitivity

SOME THINGS THAT WE KNOW OF RABBI SHIMON'S teachings and his feelings help us understand how he was spared from the moral malady that struck Rabbi Akiva's earlier disciples.

> Rabbi Shimon bar Yochai said, "It is better for a person to throw himself into a fiery furnace rather than embarrass his fellow in public" (*Berachos* 43b).
>
> Rabbi Shimon bar Yochai said that one of the things that "God hates and that I, too, do not love" is "someone who enters his own home suddenly, and surely someone who enters the home of his fellow" (*Vayikra Rabbah* 21:8).

They could not fathom how people could occupy themselves with earning a livelihood.

Rabbi Shimon's experience after emerging from hiding in the cave sheds light on the balance between striving for spiritual growth and showing consideration for others. As recounted in *Shabbos* 33b, after twelve years of exile in the cave, he and his son, Rabbi Eliezer, were informed by the prophet Elijah that the decree of death had been lifted, and their lives were no longer in danger. In the rarefied atmosphere of the cave, where they had been involved exclusively in the most profound study of the Torah and its mysteries, they could not fathom how people could occupy themselves with anything so mundane as earning a livelihood. They saw people plowing and sowing and were aghast. Wherever they cast a baleful eye, things were incinerated. A Heavenly voice rang out, "Have you emerged to destroy My world? Return to your cave!"

A year later they were permitted to emerge again. This time, Rabbi Shimon had mellowed. Rabbi Eliezer still found the banality of the world intolerable, but Rabbi Shimon [with the greater compassion that comes with advancing years (*Maharal*)] consoled his son, saying that the total devotion to Torah study of the two of them would suffice for the world, and that they need not hold everyone else to their own high standards.

The total devotion to Torah study of the two of them would suffice for the world.

A New Outlook

ON FRIDAY, THEY SAW AN ELDERLY MAN RUNNING, WITH two bundles of fragrant myrtle branches in his hand. They asked him, "What are these for?"

He responded, "They are in honor of the Sabbath."

"But wouldn't one bundle suffice?"

The man answered, "One bundle is in honor of *Zachor* [the commandment to 'remember' the Sabbath], and the other bundle is in honor of *Shamor* [the commandment to 'safeguard' the Sabbath]."

Upon hearing this, Rabbi Shimon said to his son, "Look how the Jewish people cherish the commandments!" Then both sages were appeased; no longer were they dismayed at the crassness of society.

"Look how the Jewish people cherish the commandments!"

This incident and Rabbi Shimon's teachings about sensitivity to others speak volumes. It is understandable that such a person would be appalled at the corrupted sense of values that pervade the world. Total preoccupation with plowing and sowing? As Rabbi Shimon exclaimed, "What will become of the Torah?!" (*Berachos* 33b). But then he saw an old man running with the product of his hard work in the field; to what end? To honor the Sabbath!

This was the lesson of the Omer. That man's field was planted and sown not in honor of a bank account, but in honor of God. *Of course* God could be found in the cave where the wisdom of the *Zohar* was revealed and in-

That man's field was planted and sown not in honor of a bank account, but in honor of God.

scribed, but He could also be found in the fields of people who were wise and insightful enough to see Him there. Such people had defeated the designs of the world's Hamans. Far from failing to show respect for his peers in learning, Rabbi Shimon showed his great son how to show respect for a simple farmer, who, though unlearned, knew that the Sabbath is the source of the whole week's blessing and holiness, and that its honor justifies every exertion. Israel is one nation and all its components are precious, from the Rabbi Shimons, who have no desire but Torah study, to the farmers who invest their physical activity with devotion to the Torah's commandments and love of the Sabbath.

Such people had defeated the designs of the world's Hamans.

This was the unity that brought Israel to Mount Sinai, the insight that raised Jews from the gates of contamination to the gates of holiness, the sensitivity that spared Rabbi Shimon from the pitfall of Rabbi Akiva's earlier generation of disciples. This was the Rabbi Shimon, who "ate the manna" and, alone among his peers, received the Torah of Kabbalah, and passed it on to future generations in a surge of spiritual sunlight.

This was the Rabbi Shimon, who "ate the manna" and received the Torah of Kabbalah.

Insights

The Days of Sefirah

◆§ The eighteenth day of Iyar, which is the thirty-third day of the Omer count, is known as לַ״ג בָּעוֹמֶר, *Lag (Thirty-Third) BaOmer.* It is a day of intense joy and a day which is, in essence, shrouded in mystery. Many commentators discuss the day's relationship to the complete forty-nine day period of *Sefiras HaOmer* (Counting of the Omer) which commences on the second night of Pesach and concludes on *erev* Shavuos. In fact, *Maharsha*[1] notes that Lag BaOmer marks the start of the final third of the days of *Sefirah.* Thus, before discussing the uniqueness of Lag BaOmer, we must focus briefly on the significance of the *Sefirah* period.

A Three-Stage Process

◆§ The emergence of the Jewish people as God's Chosen Nation was a three-stage process, which can be likened to an embryo developing within the womb, followed by birth and then growth.

During the Egyptian bondage, it may have appeared to the casual observer that God had forsaken the family of Abraham, Heaven forfend. In fact, God was using the "iron crucible"[2] of bondage to purify His people and make them worthy of receiving the Torah. And one who wished to see the hand of Providence at that time could have recognized it in the miraculous population explosion which the Jews experienced despite the worsening persecution.[3] Truly, the bondage was a time of development, both physically and spiritually.

The Redemption from Egypt was Israel's birth. As *Maharal* puts it, "When Israel was in Egypt and the Holy One, Blessed is He, took them out, they were surely like a fetus which had been born, as is stated in *Midrash.* [4] Therefore, their redemption could have

1. *Moed Katan* 28a.
2. *Deuteronomy* 4:20.
3. *Exodus* 1:12.
4. *Midrash Shochar Tov, Psalms* 115.

come about only through God Himself and not through an angel."[1]

A prolonged birth can encounter complications. The birth of the Jewish nation was swift, before the people could sink to the fiftieth level of spiritual impurity, a point of no return. The גִלּוּי שְׁכִינָה, *revelation of the Divine Presence,* which the Jews experienced on the night of the Exodus was essentially a gift from Heaven [אִתְעֲרוּתָא דִלְעֵלָּא, *an awakening initiated from Above*], to rescue the Jews from the morass into which they had sunk.

The next day, the second of Pesach, marked the beginning of the Exodus' final stage, for as *Ramban* writes,[2] ". . .When they came to Mount Sinai, built a Tabernacle and the Holy One, Blessed is He, returned to dwell His Presence among them, then they returned to the level of their forefathers. . . and then they were considered redeemed." After leaving Egypt, the Jews were left with the task of making themselves worthy to receive the Torah by scaling the forty-nine levels of purity, one level each day.

A Seven-Week "Chol HaMoed"

When the Temple stood, there was an obligation to offer a communal meal-offering on the sixteenth of Nissan, the second day of Pesach. The measurement of coarsely ground barley flour used was an *omer*[3]. The Torah commands[4] that on the day of this offering, the forty-nine day *"Omer"* count begin. In discussing this *mitzvah, Ramban* writes:

> . . . He commanded regarding the Festival of Matzos that it be seven sanctified days . . . and the "eighth" day [Shavuos] is sanctified like the eighth day of the [Succos] festival. The counted days in between [Pesach and Shavuos] are like the *Chol HaMoed* (Intermediary Days) between the first and eighth days of the Festival — the

1. *Gevuros Hashem* Ch. 52.
2. Preface to the Book of *Exodus.*
3. A volume equal to 43.2 eggs.
4. *Leviticus* 23:15-16.

"eighth" day here being the Day of the Giving of the Torah when He showed them His great fire and His words were heard from within the flames. This is why our Sages refer to Shavuos as *Atzeres* (Assembly),[1] for it is like the eighth day of the Succos festival which is called by this name in Scripture.[2]

At the time of the Exodus, the forty-nine days between the first day of Pesach and the revelation at Sinai were a period of preparation for the moment when all of Israel would hear the voice of the Living God. The days of *Sefirah* remain a time of spiritual striving as we prepare for the Festival of Shavuos.

Sefer HaChinuch writes that the counting toward Shavuos "demonstrates our great desire to this exalted day for which our hearts yearn. . . for when a person keeps count [until a certain day arrives] he demonstrates that his whole desire and longing is to reach that day."

The commentators note that the days of *Sefirah* are infused with a special aura and are most auspicious for spiritual growth. In a letter written during this period, R' Avraham of Sochachov, author of *Avnei Nezer,* apologized for his brevity by explaining that each moment of *Sefirah* is exceedingly precious, and therefore he was anxious to close the letter and resume his schedule of Divine service.

Sefer Chemdas HaYamim[3] writes: "During these days between Pesach and Shavuos. . . the sanctity progressively grows until the day when the Torah was given. In these days, every Jew can find Divine assistance in perfecting his soul with purity and sanctity. . . These are awesome days which stand at the pinnacle of the universe. . .."

In many communities, the nightly *Omer* count is followed by a beautiful prayer in which we beseech God:

. . . May it be Your will, HASHEM, *our God and the God of our*

---

1. See, for example, *Mishnah Succah* 5:7.

2. *Ramban* to *Leviticus* 23:36.

3. In his ethical will, R' Alexander Ziskind of Horodna, author of *Yesod V'Shoresh HaAvodah,* wrote, "First among all works of *mussar* (ethics), you should study *Sefer Chemdas Yamim.*"

forefathers, that in the merit of the Omer count that I have counted today. . . may I be cleansed and sanctified with the holiness of Above . . .

The Lesson of the Omer

You shall count for yourselves . . . from the day when you bring the Omer waving . . . (Leviticus 23:15).

◆§ The Torah's linking of the *Sefirah* count to the *Omer* offering indicates a connection between the two.

In explaining the *mitzvah* of the *Omer* offering, *Sefer HaChinuch* (§302) writes:

> Among the roots of this *mitzvah* is that we should ponder the great kindness which the Holy One, Blessed is He, does with His creatures, to renew for them, year after year, grain for sustenance. Therefore, it is fitting that we offer some of it unto the Blessed One, so that we recall His great kindness and goodness before partaking of it. And once we have made ourselves, through our deeds, fitting receptacles for blessing, our crop will be blessed and God's desire of us will be complete.

This is analagous to the requirement that one recite a blessing before partaking of any food or drink. Only after expressing our recognition that one's sustenance is a gift from God are we permitted to benefit from it. Similarly, only after presenting God, as it were, with an offering of the new crop are we permitted to partake of it. And through this symbolic act of recognition, we merit further material blessing.

The Midrash offers another symbolism inherent in the Omer offering:

> R' Yanai said: In the common way of the world, when a person buys a measure of meat in the market, he must go through great effort and difficulty until it is finally cooked. [In contrast to this,] people sleep in their beds as the Holy One, Blessed is He, makes the winds blow and the clouds

> ascend so that vegetation grows and the fruits mature — and all that the people give in return is the Omer offering![1]

R' Chaim Freidlander *(Sifsei Chaim)* explains: "The primary purpose of the *Omer* offering is so that we realize that all is from God and to recognize His providence in nature. Rain, through which vegetation sprouts, is representative of God's might — and it is for us to recognize that all this is a miracle."

Thus, the *Omer* offering is intertwined with the open miracles of the Exodus, for in the well-known words of *Ramban*:

> . . . and from the great and open miracles, one comes to recognize the hidden miracles, which are the foundation of the entire Torah. For a man has no share in the Torah of Moses until he believes that all our happenings and occurrences are miraculous — there is nothing natural in them at all.[2]

The *Omer* is also intertwined with the counting of days until Shavuos because the concepts which it represents are crucial for proper observance and study of Torah. Only through true *emunah* and *bitachon* (faith and trust in God) can one truly fulfill his Divine mission on this earth, and only through proper recognition of the great gift of Torah can a Jew observe its laws with true dedication and love *(Mishnas R' Aharon)*.

Cause for Celebration

Chasam Sofer offers the following reason to explain why Lag BaOmer is a day of celebration.[3] The Torah states: "They [Israel] journeyed from Elim, and the entire assembly of the Children of Israel arrived at the Wilderness of Sin, which is between Elim and Sinai, on the fifteenth day of the second month from their departure from the land of Egypt."[4] The "second month" is Iyar,

---

1. *Vayikra Rabbah* 28:2.
2. *Ramban* to *Exodus* 13:16
3. This reason is mentioned here because of its relevance to the concepts discussed above. Other reasons for the joy of Lag BaOmer are discussed at length in the sections that follow.
4. *Exodus* 16:1.

which immediately follows Nissan, which the Torah designates as the first month.[1] The next day, the sixteenth of Iyar, the people complained to Moses, Aaron and the elders, "If only we would have died by the hand of Hashem in the land of Egypt, as we sat by the pot of meat, when we ate bread to satiety. . ."[2] On the following day, the seventeenth of Iyar, God told Moses that manna would begin to fall from heaven on the next day, the eighteenth of Iyar, the date of Lag BaOmer.

Thus, Lag BaOmer is also a celebration of the miraculous food which demonstrated God's constant Providence over His nation and taught them "that not by bread alone does man live, rather by everything that emanates from the mouth of God does man live."[3] This idea is intertwined with the message inherent in the *Omer* count, which, as explained above, is a declaration of faith and trust in God.

The Forty-Eight Qualities

Our Sages taught that the very body of the Torah scholar is bound up with the spiritual fire of Torah.[4] For this to occur, however, the scholar must first sanctify himself by engaging in sincere character refinement and spiritual development. In fact, *tikun hamidos* (character refinement) is a precondition for proper fulfillment of all the Torah's commandments. This, says R' Chaim Vital,[5] is why character refinement is not included among the Torah's six-hundred-thirteen commandments. It precedes the commandments, for without it, the Torah cannot be observed properly.

The Mishnah[6] lists forty-eight qualities through which the gift of Torah is acquired. Among them are: *attentive listening, reverence, modesty, purity, slowness to anger, a good heart, faith in*

1. *Exodus* 12:2.
2. Ibid. 16:3.
3. *Deuteronomy* 8:3.
4. *Chagigah* 27a.
5. *Shaarei Kedushah* 1:2.
6. *Avos* 6:6.

Torah leaders, loving justice and feeling another Jew's plight. R' Chaim Volozhiner stated that one's attainment of Torah knowledge is in exact proportion to his efforts in acquiring these forty-eight qualities. For just as in monetary matters, a Jew cannot acquire without a method of *kinyan,* acquisition, that is specified by the Torah, so too, a student cannot acquire the gift of Torah if he lacks the methods of acquisition enumerated by our Sages. The first forty-eight days of the *Sefirah* period correspond to the forty-eight qualities through which Torah is acquired. The forty-ninth day, the eve of Shavuos, is a sacred day when each Jew, having striven to develop the forty-eight qualities within himself, can prepare for the awesome moment in time when the Torah was given at Sinai *(Mishnas R' Aharon).*

Sefiros/Emanations

⁂ Man can have no conception of God Himself, for His true being is beyond human intelligence. All we can know are His manifestations, the various ways in which He seems to behave towards us, such as mercy, power, judgment, etc. Even these can come to us only through intermediaries, for we can never perceive God's essence.

The writings of Kabbalah refer to these intermediaries as the *Sefiros,* which in this context is generally translated as *Emanations.* Each one of the *Sefiros* corresponds to a great Biblical personality who personified that particular trait, and the order of the *Sefiros* is as follows:

חֶסֶד, *Lovingkindness* — represented by Abraham;
גְבוּרָה, *Power* — Isaac;
תִּפְאֶרֶת, *Splendor* — Jacob;
נֶצַח, *Eternity* — Moses;
הוֹד, *Glory* — Aaron;
יְסוֹד, *Foundation* — Joseph
מלכות, *Kingship* — David.

Each one of the *Sefiros* also combines with the others; e.g. חֶסֶד שֶׁבְּחֶסֶד, חֶסֶד שֶׁבִּגְבוּרָה, חֶסֶד שֶׁבְּתִפְאֶרֶת . . ., resulting in a total of forty-nine Emanations. The masters of Kabbalah taught that the seven weeks of *Sefirah* (which in its plain meaning is translated *counting*) correspond to these *Sefiros*/Emanations, beginning with חֶסֶד שֶׁבְּחֶסֶד on the first day and concluding with מַלְכוּת שֶׁבְּמַלְכוּת on the forty-ninth.

The *Sefiros* exist in man's personal world as well. A Jew is commanded to emulate the ways of His Creator and that includes developing himself in these forty-nine ways. For example, when a person's sense of responsibility motivates him to organize charity projects, his actions are illustrative of חֶסֶד שֶׁבִּגְבוּרָה, *kindness within strength*. One who fails in this area has shown himself lacking in this particular trait. On each day of the *Sefirah* period, one should strive to develop in himself that day's *emanation-trait*.

In the beautiful prayer which many recite following the *Omer* count, one prays: ". . .In the merit of the Omer count that I have counted today, may there be corrected whatever blemish I have caused in the *Sefirah* (Emanation). . . May I be cleansed and sanctified with the holiness of Above. . ."

Glory within Glory

The day of Lag BaOmer corresponds to הוֹד שֶׁבְּהוֹד, *glory within glory*. The commentators see great significance in this in a variety of ways. *Chidushei HaRim* states that Lag BaOmer is auspicious for attaining *yiras Shamayim*, awe of Heaven. R' Gedaliah Schorr (*Ohr Gedalyahu*) explained that the primary *glory* of a person is that which he accomplishes through his toil and effort. Our Sages teach, "All is in the hands of Heaven, save for [attaining] awe of Heaven."[1] Whether a person will be rich or poor, weak or strong, is Divinely ordained, but awe of Heaven is entirely in the hands of the individual. Moreover, "The beginning of wisdom is awe of God."[2]

The Talmud states[3] that a scholar who acquires Torah wisdom but lacks fear of Heaven is like a treasurer who is given keys to

1. *Berachos* 33b.
2. Psalms 111:10.
3. *Shabbos* 31a.

an inner vault but not the keys to an outer chamber through which one gains access to the vault. Obviously, the treasurer will never reach the vault. Similarly, Torah knowledge is the inner secret of God's essence and will. Awe of God is the prerequisite (outer chamber) for true perception of God's will.

Thus, Lag BaOmer is a crucial prelude to the festival of Shavuous when we relive the giving of the Torah at Sinai and renew our commitment to Torah.

As mentioned above, the *Sefirah* of הוד, *glory,* is associated with Aaron, who served as *Kohen Gadol* (High Priest). Aaron's primary *glory* was that which he bore within his heart. "The heart that was glad about his brother's greatness will wear the *Urim V'Tumim*" [the Ineffable Name of God which was contained in the *Kohen Gadol's* Breastplate].[1] This refers to Aaron's gladness over the fact that Moses, his younger brother, had been chosen over himself as prophet and redeemer of his people.[2]

Hillel the Elder taught: "Be among the disciples of Aaron, loving peace and pursuing peace, loving people and bringing them closer to Torah."[3] Aaron showed kindness to everyone. If someone did not know how to pray or recite *Shema,* Aaron would teach him. If a person had difficulty understanding Torah, Aaron would study with him.[4] Moreover, he went to great lengths to resolve marital disputes and other instances of strife.[5]

As mentioned above, the first forty-eight days of the *Sefirah* period correspond to the forty-eight qualities through which Torah is acquired. According to one opinion, the thirty-third quality is אוֹהֵב אֶת הַצְּדָקוֹת, *loving righteous ways. Tiferes Yisrael* explains: "Not only will [one with this trait] minimize the [social and moral] obligations of others towards him and maximize his obligation towards them, but. . . his heart will ache exceedingly

1. *Shemos Rabbah* 3:17.
2. See *Exodus* 4:14.
3. *Avos* 1:12.
4. *Tana D'Vei Eliyahu* Ch. 13.
5. *Avos D'R'Nosson* 12:3.

when people are harming one another. . ." How appropriate that this trait should correspond to Lag BaOmer, the day of *Glory within Glory,* the essence of Aaron.

Rabbi Akiva and His Disciples

Cessation of Mourning

The commentators provide a number of reasons for Lag BaOmer's status as a day of celebration.

As the Talmud relates,[1] during the *Sefirah* period, twenty-four thousand disciples of the Talmudic sage Rabbi Akiva died, for they did not accord one another proper respect.[2] It is for this reason that a period of mourning is observed during *Sefirah.* Weddings are prohibited, as are haircuts (as in the first weeks of mourning following the death of a close relative), and it is customary to refrain from playing music or engaging in other forms of merriment.[3]

There are varying traditions as to the exact period within *Sefirah* when these deaths occurred. This diversity is the source for the differing customs as to when the mourning period is ob-

1. *Yevamos* 62b.

2. R' Aharon Kotler (*Mishnas R' Aharon,* Vol. III, pp. 13 and 17) and R' Yehudah Zev Segal (*Inspiration and Insight,* Vol. I, p. 193) note that the spiritual levels of Rabbi Akiva's disciples were undoubtedly great, and their sin must be understood in this context. They surely accorded one another respect *by our standards.* The righteous, however, are judged according to their own spiritual level.

3. *Taz* (493:2) states another reason for mourning during the *Sefirah* period: the worst massacres of the Crusades happened in the weeks between Pesach and Shavuos. It was the custom of some communities to recite special prayers on the Sabbaths of the *Sefirah* period in commemoration of these tragic events; some of the *Kinnos* recited on Tishah B'Av focus on these tragedies.

Another reason cited for the restrictions on weddings and other joyous celebrations during this period is that in Kabbalistic thought, *Sefirah* is a time of Divine judgment; see *Chok Yaakov, Orach Chaim* 493:3.

The laws and customs of the *Sefirah* period are found in *Shulchan Aruch, Orach Chaim* Ch. 493.

served.[1] In his *Beis HaBechirah,* R' Menachem *HaMeiri* cites a tradition[2] that the deaths of Rabbi Akiva's disciples ceased on the day of *Lag BaOmer,* "and for this reason it is customary to refrain from fasting on that day."[3] This is the opinion held by *Rama* who therefore rules that "there is an increase, to some extent, of joy, and *Tachanun* is not recited."[4]

The author of *Shulchan Aruch,* Rabbi Yosef Karo, follows the tradition that the deaths stopped on the thirty-fourth day of *Sefirah.* Even according to this tradition, there are reasons why Lag BaOmer is celebrated as a day of special joy, as will be explained.

A Time for Respect

⁂ The essence of Lag BaOmer makes it particularly appropriate for rejoicing over the cessation of deaths of R' Akiva's disciples — deaths which were the result of the disciples not according one another proper respect.

As mentioned above, Lag BaOmer corresponds to the *Sefirah*/ Emanation of הוֹד שֶׁבְּהוֹד, *Glory within Glory.* The trait which this *Sefirah* represents was embodied by Aaron, the man who symbolized peace and unity among Jews. *Avos D'R'Nosson* (12:3) relates that the key to Aaron's great success in settling strife and inspiring repentance was the respect which he accorded one and all. He would extend greetings to a wicked person when meeting him in the street, and later, the person would say to himself, "How will I be able to greet Aaron if I commit this sin? I would be ashamed to face him!"

The Sages further state that Aaron never rebuked with strong words. His words were always spoken with love and respect. In this way, his words had their intended effect and he earned the love and admiration of all.

Thus, inherent in Lag BaOmer is the message of respect for all. Certainly those who devote themselves to the study of

1. See Laws and Customs, p. 96.
2. This tradition is found also in another early commentator, *Sefer HaManhig* §106.
3. *Meiri* to *Yevamos* 62b.
4. *Orach Chaim* 493:2.

Torah and embody its teachings must be treated with honor and dignity, by others and by one another.

Maharal notes that Lag BaOmer falls on the eighteenth of Iyar. The word חַי, *life,* has the numerical value of 18, and the numerical value of אִיָּיר, *Iyar,* is identical with that of אֹרֶךְ, *length,* as in אֹרֶךְ יָמִים בִּימִינָהּ, *Length of days are in her [the Torah's] right hand.*[1] The day of Lag BaOmer symbolizes that when Torah and its students are accorded proper respect, the result is *life* and *length of days.*

The Opinion of Pri Chadash

Pri Chadash wonders why the cessation of the deaths of Rabbi Akiva's disciples should be cause for celebration, for does not the Talmud state that as a result of their deaths "the world became [spiritually] desolate"?[2] He therefore suggests that the real cause for celebration is the fact that after his disciples' deaths, "Rabbi Akiva came to our Sages in the south and taught them. [They were:] Rabbi Meir, Rabbi Yehudah, Rabbi Yosei, Rabbi Shimon [bar Yochai], and Rabbi Elazar ben Shamua. It was they who preserved the Torah at that time."[3] There is a tradition[4] that it was on the day of Lag BaOmer when Rabbi Akiva began teaching Torah to these five disciples.

At the time of his disciples' deaths, R' Akiva was well advanced in years.[5] Surely his pain and sorrow at their deaths was enormous. A lesser man would have fallen prey to despair. Yet R' Akiva mustered his strength of body and spirit and carried on his mission as transmitter of Torah and leader of his generation.

In the words of R' Gedaliah Schorr:

> Lag BaOmer is a day on which to strengthen oneself in the area of Torah study. Even if one has not learned properly, and has had periods of failure, on Lag BaOmer he should strengthen himself and take a lesson from R' Akiva. After

---

1. *Proverbs* 3:16.
2. *Yevamos* 62b.
3. Ibid.
4. See *Kaf HaChayim, Orach Chaim* 493:26 and *Sefer Chagim U'Zmanim — Lag BaOmer.*
5. He began to teach Torah at age eighty.

twenty-four thousand of his disciples died, he developed five new disciples, among them R' Shimon Bar Yochai, and it was through them that Torah was disseminated among Israel. Just as Rabbi Akiva did not despair, so too, a Jew should not let past failures and difficult situations lead him to despair; rather, he should immerse himself in Torah with renewed strength *(Ohr Gedalyahu).*[1]

Some have a custom to visit the grave of R' Akiva on Lag BaOmer. The *Ben Ish Chai,* citing Kabbalistic sources, writes that the soul of R' Akiva rejoices on this day. Let us briefly discuss the qualities of this great sage.

Love of God

Shir HaShirim (Song of Songs) is an allegory depicting the love between God and the Jewish people. It was Rabbi Akiva who said, "All [Scriptural] Songs are holy, but Song of Songs is holiest of holy."[2] *Zohar Chadash* relates that Rabbi Akiva's disciples once found him reciting *Shir HaShirim* on the Sabbath day with tears flowing down his cheeks as he was overcome with intense love of God. His disciples questioned him, "Our teacher, did you not teach us, 'If you proclaim the Sabbath a delight. . .'[3] [and isn't crying a contradiction to this]?" Rabbi Akiva replied, "This *is* my delight."[4]

There was no greater testimony to Rabbi Akiva's intense love of God than at his life's end, when he recited the *Shema,* accepting God's sovereignty, as the Romans tore his flesh with hot combs. He was joyous, oblivious to the pain. Turnus Rufus, the Roman commander who ordered the barbarous execution, was flabbergasted. "Have you no feeling of pain, that you can laugh in the face of such intense suffering?"Even Rabbi Akiva's disciples wondered, "Our teacher, even to this extent?"

The dying sage explained, "All my life I was concerned over a

1. This point is also discussed in *Inspiration and Insight* (Discourses on the weekly *parashah* by R' Yehudah Zev Segal), p. 198.
2. Mishnah *Yadayim* 3:5.
3. *Isaiah* 58:13.
4. *Zohar Chadash* cited by *Mishnah Berurah* 288:4.

phrase in the Torah. We are taught in the Torah to accept God's sovereignty and decrees upon ourselves בְּכָל נַפְשְׁךָ, *with all your soul* — even if He takes your life. I used to wonder if I would ever have the privilege of serving God to such a degree. Now that the opportunity has come to me, shall I not grasp it with joy?"

He recited the first verse of *Shema — Hear O Israel,* HASHEM *is our God,* HASHEM *the One and Only* — and he drew out the word אֶחָד, *One,* until his soul left him.

A Heavenly voice proclaimed: "You are praiseworthy, Rabbi Akiva, for your soul left you as you proclaimed God's Oneness! . . . You are praiseworthy, Rabbi Akiva, for you are fit to enter the life of the World to Come."[1]

Thus, Rabbi Akiva attained the highest levels of pure faith and love of God. An outgrowth of אֱמוּנָה, *faith,* is בִּטָחוֹן, *trust,* in God. After suffering the massive loss of his 24,000 disciples, Rabbi Akiva lived with ironclad faith that whatever transpires is a result of God's will and that God's promise that the Torah would never be forgotten from Israel[2] would be realized. Surely he possessed the trust that with God at his side, he could succeed, even at his advanced age, at planting the seeds of Torah knowledge in a desolate world and that his new disciples would grow to become mighty trees of Torah wisdom.

Love of Torah

Zohar states: "Israel, the Torah, and the Holy One, Blessed is He, are One." In discussing the *mitzvah* of loving God, *Sefer HaChinuch* writes that the only way to arrive at an authentic appreciation of God is by intensively studying the teachings of His Torah. When one focuses his mind on the Torah with total concentration, love for God will penetrate his heart.

Until age 40, Rabbi Akiva was ignorant of Torah. He was inspired to study Torah when he observed how water could wear grooves into solid stone after years of constant dripping. He said to himself, "If soft water can penetrate hard stone, certainly the

1. *Berachos* 61b; *Yerushalmi Berachos* 9:5.
2. *Deuteronomy* 31:21.

iron-strong Torah can leave its imprint on my heart."[1] Rabbi Akiva attained incredible heights in Torah; his teachings are considered the very foundations of the Oral Law.

The Talmud states, "If Israel had not sinned, they would have been given only the Five Books of the Torah and the Book of *Joshua*."[2] This means that they would have been able to derive from the Five Books all the teachings found in the remaining books of Scripture and in the Oral Law. In fact, the Talmud relates that Rabbi Akiva's greatness in Torah was such that he derived mounds and mounds of laws from every point of every letter in the Torah. When Moses, the humblest of men, was shown the greatness of Rabbi Akiva, he asked, "A man such as this is to be found and you are giving the Torah through me?"[3]

Sefer HaChinuch writes: "One Who truly loves God will surely strive to share his passion with others and will do all he can to teach them about the Almighty, as we find in the case of our Patriarch Abraham."

Rabbi Akiva, whose love of God and greatness in Torah was unsurpassed in his day, overcame incredible trials and tribulations to transmit God's teachings to the next generation.

Love of One's Fellow Jew

Rabbi Akiva said:
" 'You shall love your fellow as yourself'[4] — This is a great rule in the Torah."[5]

Every Jewish soul is represented by a letter in the Torah. The word יִשְׂרָאֵל (Israel) forms the initial letters of יֵשׁ שִׁשִּׁים רִבּוֹא אוֹתִיּוֹת לַתּוֹרָה, *There are 600,000 letters in the Torah*,[6] while another name of the Jewish people, יְשֻׁרוּן *(Jeshurun)*,[7] forms the initials of

1. *Avos D'R' Nosson* 6:2.
2. *Nedarim* 22b.
3. *Menachos* 29b. This point is discussed in *Ohr Gedalyahu.*
4. *Leviticus* 19:18.
5. *Rashi* ad loc. citing *Toras Kohanim.*
6. *Zohar Chadash* to *Shir HaShirim.*
7. See *Deuteronomy* 33:5 and 33:26.

יֵשׁ שִׁשִּׁים רִבּוֹא נְשָׁמוֹת, *There are 600,000 [Jewish] souls.*[1] As Rabbi Akiva demonstrated, there is infinite wisdom hidden within each letter of the Torah. Furthermore, each letter is unique, no two letters convey the same teachings. In a similar sense, no two souls are alike, and like the crowns which adorn the letters of a Torah scroll, every Jewish soul is crowned with some special quality which, in that area, makes it unique.[2]

In discussing the blessing recited at the conclusion of the Torah reading, *Shulchan Aruch*[3] writes that the words אֲשֶׁר נָתַן לָנוּ תּוֹרַת אֱמֶת, *Who has given us a Torah of truth,* refers to the Written Torah, while וְחַיֵּי עוֹלָם נָטַע בְּתוֹכֵנוּ, *and Who has implanted within us eternal life,* refers to the Oral Torah. Rabbi Akiva was outstanding in his love of every Jew and perceived the hidden qualities of every Jewish soul. Through this attachment, he discovered the hidden treasures of Oral teachings contained within the letters of the Torah, letters which represent the souls of the Jewish people.

As mentioned above, perfection of *midos,* character traits, is a prerequisite for attaching oneself to the Torah and plumbing its depths. In addition to its obvious meaning, Rabbi Akiva's teaching that *ahavas Yisrael,* love of one's fellow Jew, is "a great rule in the Torah," also means that it is primary among the qualities needed for success in Torah learning (R' Moshe Wolfson in *Emunas Itecha*).

---

1. In fact, there are far less than 600,000 letters in the Torah and far more than 600,000 Jews. With regard to the Torah's letters, *Chasam Sofer* and *Pri Tzaddik* both explain that certain letters of the Hebrew alphabet are actually combinations of other letters. For example, the upper-right segment of the letter א is a י; the lower-left segment is a י; and these two segments are connected by a diagonal ו.

The Jewish people are represented by the 600,000 men who departed Egypt and who stood at the foot of Mount Sinai to receive the Torah. Every Jewish soul is rooted in a letter of the Torah.

2. Every Jewish soul has its own unique *chein,* grace, through which it finds favor before God. The quality which earns it this favor is hidden from everyone; if one will seek and discover that he is blessed with a particular quality and will decide it is *that* quality which makes him unique and favorable before God, he can be certain that such is not the case. For his uniqueness is hidden and concealed and no man can perceive it (R' Moshe Wolfson in *Emunas Itecha,* citing *Chidushei HaRim*).

3. *Orach Chaim* 139:10.

The Song of Rabbi Akiva

A popular Lag BaOmer song is taken from a statement by Rabbi Akiva concerning repentance, found in the concluding *mishnah* of Tractate *Yoma:*

> אָמַר רַבִּי עֲקִיבָא: אַשְׁרֵיכֶם יִשְׂרָאֵל – לִפְנֵי מִי אַתֶּם מִטַּהֲרִין? מִי מְטַהֵר אֶתְכֶם? אֲבִיכֶם שֶׁבַּשָּׁמַיִם. . . וְאוֹמֵר: "מִקְוֵה יִשְׂרָאֵל ה' " – מָה מִקְוֶה מְטַהֵר אֶת הַטְּמֵאִים אַף הַקָּדוֹשׁ בָּרוּךְ הוּא מְטַהֵר אֶת יִשְׂרָאֵל.
> *Rabbi Akiva said: "Praiseworthy are you, O Israel! Before Whom do you cleanse yourselves? Who cleanses you? Your Father in Heaven! . . . And He says: 'The mikveh of Israel is* HASHEM.'[1] *Just as a mikveh purifies the contaminated, so does the Holy One, Blessed is He, purify Israel."*

The thought expressed by R' Akiva coincides beautifully with the purpose of the *Sefirah* period, a period of spiritual cleansing in preparation for the Festival of the Giving of the Torah. "Before Whom do you cleanse yourselves?" Before God, Who asks only that we take the initial step toward Him before He extends His help to us and ensures that our efforts at self-improvement will succeed. God calls to us, "Open for me an opening the size of a needle's eye and I will open for you an opening the size of a large hall."[2] In this way, the process of *teshuvah,* return to God, is like immersion in a *mikveh* : one need only to submerge himself in the *mikveh* and the waters will purify him. Similarly, one need only demonstrate a sincere desire to rejuvenate himself spiritually and God will be there to cleanse him.

Ahavas Hashem, love of Hashem, and *ahavas Yisrael,* love of one's fellow Jew, are intertwined. It is through recognition of the חֵלֶק אֱלֹקַ מִמַּעַל, the Heavenly spark in every Jewish soul, that one can overlook another's faults and develop a feeling of genuine love and esteem toward him.

The question has been asked: If the Torah commands us to

---

1. *Jeremiah* 17:13.
2. *Shir HaShirim Rabbah* 5:3.

love God with *all our heart,*[1] then how can we be commanded to also channel our love toward our fellow Jew? Are we not required to direct *all* our love toward our Creator? The answer to this is: love of one's fellow Jew is an extension of one's love of God. This is alluded to in the Torah's concluding the command to love one's fellow Jew with the words *I am* HASHEM.[2]

It is remarkable, notes R' Moshe Wolfson, that the *gematria* (numerical value) of וְאָהַבְתָּ אֵת ה׳ אֱלֹקֶיךָ *(And you shall love* HASHEM*, your God)* is equal to that of וְאָהַבְתָּ לְרֵעֲךָ כָּמוֹךָ אֲנִי ה׳ *(Love your fellow as yourself — I am* HASHEM*)* — 907.

"Praiseworthy are you, O Israel! Before Whom do you cleanse yourselves? Who cleanses you? Your Father in Heaven! . . .And He says: 'The mikveh of Israel is HASHEM*.' "* In this verse, the word מִקְוֵה, *mikveh,* in its plain translation means *hope*. The term can also mean *ingathering.*[3] The hope and assurance of Israel's ultimate redemption lies in its relationship with God, a relationship which unites the Jewish people with their Creator and with each other.

Tzaddikim of earlier generations taught that on Lag BaOmer, which marks the start of the final third of the *Sefirah* period, the aura of Shavuos begins to manifest itself. How appropriate that "the song of Rabbi Akiva" is sung on that day. The declaration of נַעֲשֶׂה וְנִשְׁמָע, *"We will do and we will listen,"*[4] with which the Jewish people announced their willingness to accept the Torah, was rooted in pure love of God. But, as *Ohr HaChaim* notes, they would not have been deemed worthy of receiving the Torah had they not arrived at Sinai with total unity, *like one man with one heart.*[5] The spirited singing of R' Akiva's teaching should infuse us with love of Hashem and love for one another.

---

1. *Deuteronomy* 6:5.

2. *Leviticus* 19:18.

3. As in יִקָּווּ הַמַּיִם, *Let the waters be gathered (Genesis* 1:9). The term מִקְוֶה, *mikveh,* in its literal sense means *a gathering of water.*

4. *Exodus* 24:7.

5. *Rashi* to *Exodus* 19:2.

Rabbi Shimon bar Yochai

A True Disciple

⁂ One of the five "Sages of the south" who became Rabbi Akiva's disciples and transmitted the Torah to the next generation[1] was Rabbi Shimon bar Yochai, who departed this world on the eighteenth of Iyar, the day of Lag BaOmer.[2]

R' Shimon lived during the tumultuous years at the end of the Second Temple era and immediately following the Temple's destruction. His attachment to his teacher, R' Akiva, is evident from a number of Talmudic passages. *Talmud Yerushalmi*[3] relates that upon appointing two disciples to the *Sanhedrin* (Supreme Court), R' Akiva sat R' Meir ahead of R' Shimon, for R' Meir was older. R' Shimon, not realizing the real reason for this arrangement, felt chagrined for, in his humility, he took this as a sign of R' Akiva's lack of regard for him. Realizing this, R' Akiva told him, "It is sufficient that I and your Creator recognize your strength [i.e. your spiritual qualities]."

In commenting on the above, R' Yeshaya Asher Zelig Margulies writes:

> Take note of the greatness of our Sages' remarks, for the word of God was in the mouth of Rabbi Akiva in a literal sense when he spoke those words to R' Shimon, who was then in his youth. At that time, the essential spiritual strength and power, the awesome and sacred might of R' Shimon bar Yochai was still concealed within him, the lamp of God upon his head which would yet cast its glow upon the entire world had not yet been revealed. Yet his

1. See p. 36.

2. *Bnei Yissoschor* (*Chodesh Iyar* 3:4) asserts that the eighteenth of Iyar is also R' Shimon bar Yochai's birthdate, "for the Holy One, Blessed is He, completes the years of the righteous as we find by Moses, whose birth and death were both on the seventh of Adar." *Bnei Yissoschor* may be alluding to the Kabbalistic tradition (found in the writings of the *Arizal* and other sources) that R' Shimon bar Yochai's soul was a *nitzutz* (spark) of that of Moses.

3. *Sanhedrin* 1:2.

holy teacher R' Akiva, of whom it was said, "Blessed is HASHEM, the G-d of Israel, Who revealed His secrets to R' Akiva ben Yosef"[1]. . . recognized his strength (preface to *Kocho D'Rashbi*).

The Talmud relates that in the years following the Second Temple's destruction, the Romans issued harsh decrees against their Jewish subjects in the Land of Israel. Rabbi Akiva defied the decree banning the teaching of Torah and was later tortured to death. During Rabbi Akiva's imprisonment, he was visited by R' Shimon who, risking his life, implored Rabbi Akiva to teach him Torah.[2] R' Akiva told him, "More than the calf wishes to suck, the cow wishes to suckle," meaning that his desire to teach R' Shimon was even greater than R' Shimon's desire to learn from him, but R' Akiva did not want to endanger his disciple's life. To this, R' Shimon replied, "But who is in danger? Is it not the calf who is in danger?" meaning that he was willing to take the risk, whereupon R' Akiva conveyed a number of teachings to him.

R' Tzadok HaKohen of Lublin *(Pri Tzaddik)* suggests that it would have been fitting to celebrate the *yahrtzeit* of R' Akiva, whose teachings, as mentioned above, are the foundation of the Oral Law. However, the tragic circumstances surrounding his death make celebration on that day impossible. Instead, we combine the celebration of R' Akiva's teachings with that of his disciple R' Shimon, who once told his own disciples, "My sons, study my teachings, because my teachings are the cream of the cream [the most select] of R' Akiva's teachings." [3]

In the Cave with R' Elazar

R' Shimon bar Yochai's command of the revealed portion of the Oral Law was formidable, and evoked unusual expressions of praise: "R' Shimon is worthy enough to be relied upon in a time

1. *Kallah Rabasi* 3.
2. *Pesachim* 122a.
3. *Gittin* 67a.

of emergency'';[1] ''We extend our graciousness to R' Shimon'';[2] and ''One whose mother is giving birth should pray that she give birth [to a child] like R' Shimon. . .''[3] His literary legacy includes all the anonymous statements in *Sifri*[4] and the *Mechilta of Rashbi,*[5] only part of which is extant.

By R' Shimon's own testimony, his unfathomable heights in Torah wisdom, in which its secrets were unlocked and lay revealed before him, were attained through his total immersion in study under conditions which were at once incredibly trying and miraculous. It was during a thirteen year period in which he hid in a cave with his son R' Elazar that R' Shimon achieved his *shleimus,* spiritual perfection, and the secrets of the Torah which form the basis of the classic work of *Kabbalah, Sefer HaZohar,* were revealed to him.[6]

The Talmud relates:[7]

> It happened once that R' Yehudah, R' Yose and R' Shimon bar Yochai were sitting together, and Yehudah ben Geirim[8] was sitting next to them. R' Yehudah opened the discussion and said: ''How admirable are the deeds of the Romans [who ruled the Land of Israel at that time]! Throughout the Land they have established marketplaces, bridges and even bathhouses!''
>
> Upon hearing R' Yehudah's praise of the Roman occupation, R' Yose remained silent. R' Shimon bar Yochai, however, answered him and said, ''Everything they established, they established only to serve their own needs.

1. *Berachos* 9a.
2. *Bava Metzia* 119a.
3. *Makkos* 17b.
4. A halachic Midrash on *Numbers* and *Deuteronomy.*
5. On the Book of *Exodus*. רשב״י, *Rashbi,* is an acronym for רבי שמעון בר יוחאי.
6. Introduction to *Zohar.*
7. *Shabbos* 33b. The elucidated translation which follows is drawn from the Schottenstein Edition of *Talmud Bavli,* as are accompanying footnotes, except for those from *Midos Rashbi.* A supplement to this Talmudic account, drawn from *Zohar,* appears on pp. 127-129.
8. So named because he was the son of *geirim,* proselytes *(Rashi).*

They established marketplaces for immoral purposes, bathhouses to beautify themselves, and bridges to collect tolls."

R' Yehudah ben Geirim, who witnessed the exchange between these Sages, went and repeated it to some of his associates[1] and eventually, reports of the conversation reached the governing authorities. They proclaimed the followed decree:

"Yehudah, who praised the Romans, shall be elevated. Yose, who remained silent, shall be exiled to the town of Tzippori.[2] Shimon, who denigrated the Romans, shall be executed."

R' Shimon and his son R' Elazar fled and hid in a *beis midrash*. Every day, R' Shimon's wife would bring them bread and a small jug of water. But when the Romans intensified their search, R' Shimon became concerned lest the Romans coerce his wife into revealing their hiding place.

With this in mind, R' Shimon and his son hid in a cave. A miracle occurred — a carob tree[3] and a spring of water were created for them, and they drew their sustenance from these sources. Each day they would remove their clothing and cover

---

1. He repeated it to his parents, or to his students. His intent was not malicious and he certainly did not inform the Romans directly of the conversation. Nevertheless, word of the exchange eventually reached the ears of the authorities, as the Talmud proceeds to recount (*Rashi;* see also *Tosafos;* cf. *Anaf Yosef*) Despite his innocuous intentions, his words constituted *lashon hara,* evil speech (see *Sefer Chofetz Chaim, Hilchos Lashon Hara* 2:2-5 with *Be'er Mayim Chaim* ad loc. 3,12; see also *Cheshek Shlomo*).

For an explanation of why these Sages were having this discussion and why R' Yehudah praised the Romans, see *Maharsha, Sefas Emes, Chasam Sofer* and *Dibros Moshe* 26:92.

2. Tzippori was a town in Galilee that later became the seat of the *Sanhedrin* under R' Yehudah HaNasi (see *Rosh Hashanah* 31b).

3. *Maharsha* comments that the creation of the carob tree represented a "miracle within a miracle," for under normal circumstances it takes seventy years for a carob tree to bear its first fruits (see *Taanis* 23a). Here, however, the fruit was provided immediately.

Midos Rashbi, citing *Midrash Talpios,* cites an authortative tradition that the carob tree would become transformed into a date tree every *erev Shabbos.* Support for this can be found in *Esther Rabbah* 3:7.

themselves with sand up to their necks as they immersed themselves in the study of Torah. They did this so that their clothing would not wear out; they donned their clothing only for prayer.

They lived this way for twelve years. Then, on a certain day, Elijah the prophet stood at the mouth of the cave and said, "Who will inform the son of Yochai that the Caesar has died and his decree is annulled?"[1] R' Shimon and his son then emerged from the cave.

As they ventured back to civilization, they passed by some people who were plowing and sowing a field. Distressed by this, R' Shimon declared, "These people are forsaking the pursuit of the World to Come and are occupying themselves instead with this transitory world!"[2] Thereafter, everywhere R' Shimon and his son would cast their gaze would immediately be incinerated.[3] Finally, a Heavenly voice rang out and proclaimed, "Have you emerged from seclusion in order to destroy My world? Return to your cave!"

They returned to their cave and dwelled there another year. At that point they said to themselves, "The sentence for evildoers in Gehinnom is no more than twelve months."[4] They felt, therefore, that their own sentence might have expired as well. A Heavenly voice then proclaimed, "Emerge from your cave!"

They emerged from their cave and again encountered people seeking their livelihood through ordinary means. This time, how-

---

1. Though Elijah visited R' Shimon and his son often during their years in the cave, he did not inform them directly that they could now leave. This may be because Elijah knew that they were destined to return to the cave for another year (*Midos Rashbi* citing *Chida* in *Pesach Einayim*).

2. That is, they are forsaking the study of Torah in favor of pursuing a livelihood. R' Shimon bar Yochai advocated the position that one who devotes his life to the pursuit of God's will, will find himself sustained by God; he need not labor unduly to provide his needs (see *Rashi;* see p. 72 in this volume).

3. Because of their towering spiritual stature, everything they perceived as evil simply ceased to exist.

4. The source for this is an exegetical reading of *Isaiah* 66:23-24, as cited in *Seder Olam* ch. 6 (*Rashi*). A similar derivation is found in Mishnah *Ediyos* 2:10 (see *Raavad* there).

ever, everything which R' Elazar destroyed through his fiery gaze, R' Shimon, his father, restored. R' Shimon told R' Elazar, "My son, the world has enough total devotees in Torah in you and me alone; we need not hold others to our standard of devotion and diligence."

Late Friday afternoon, R' Shimon and his son saw an old man who was clutching two bundles of myrtles, and was running home with them as twilight descended. When they asked him what the myrtles were for, he replied, "They are in honor of the Sabbath."[1] They questioned, "But could you not have sufficed with one bundle?" He answered them, "One is for *zachor* and one is for *shamor*."[2] Hearing this, R' Shimon said to his son, "Look how cherished the *mitzvos* are to the Jewish people" — and they were appeased.

Aruch HaShulchan (493:7) cites a tradition that it was on the day of Lag BaOmer when R' Shimon and his son R' Elazar emerged from the cave. In any event, the miraculous rescue of R' Shimon and his son from the decree of death which had been issued against them is surely cause for rejoicing and is yet another reason for the joy of Lag BaOmer *(Shei'los U'Teshuvos Lev Aryeh)*.

Above this World

The Torah relates that when Moses ascended to Heaven to receive the Torah, he spent forty days there in which he neither ate nor drank.[3] Had God willed it, Moses could have been taught all of Torah in a single day. However, for Moses to be worthy of his role

---

1. He was bringing them home so that he and his household could smell their pleasant scent on the Sabbath (*Rashi*).

2. In the Ten Commandments, God enjoined the Jewish people to *remember (zachor)* and *observe (shamor)* the Sabbath day (see *Exodus* 20:8 and *Deuteronomy* 5:12, respectively). Each of these words denotes a different aspect of Sabbath observance — *zachor* connoting the obligation to sanctify the day through acts such as the recital of *Kiddush,* and *shamor* connoting the obligation not to perform labor on the Sabbath (see *Berachos* 20b with *Rashi*).

3. *Exodus* 34:28. See "A Spark of Moses" on p. 58.

as student of God and teacher of His wisdom to the Jewish people, it was necessary that he totally subjugate his earthly desires. Only someone whose every fiber yearned for nothing but spirituality could be the one to receive and transmit the spiritual wisdom of Torah.

The same was true of R' Shimon bar Yochai. Providence arranged that a decree of death should be issued against R' Shimon, forcing him to spend thirteen years in a cave, for it was there that he would become transformed into a being worthy of being shown the Torah's most esoteric teachings. "In rocky caves where you stayed — there you acquired your glory and your strength" (from the *"Bar Yochai"* song[1]).

Given the above, we can better understand the next part of the Talmudic account of R' Shimon's emergence from the cave:

> R' Pinchas ben Yair, the son-in-law of R' Shimon,[2] heard that R' Shimon had emerged from hiding and went out to greet him. He later escorted him into the bathhouse and was massaging his flesh, when he saw that there were cracks in R' Shimon's skin. Seeing these vestiges of the years spent in the abrasive sand, R' Pinchas began to cry. As tears trickled from his eyes, they fell upon the cracks in R' Shimon's skin and caused him to cry out in pain.[3] R' Pinchas ben Yair said to his father-in-law, "Woe unto me for having seen you like this!" R' Shimon replied, "On the contrary! Fortunate are you for having seen me like this, for had you not seen me in such a state, you would have not found within me the level of Torah knowledge which I now possess." Prior to his years of seclusion, when R' Shimon bar Yochai would pose a question, R' Pinchas ben Yair would respond with twelve possible solutions. However, after R' Shimon's years in the cave, when R' Pinchas would pose a question, R' Shimon would respond with twenty-four possible solutions.

---

1. See p. 158.

2. *Melo HaRo'im* cites a source in *Zohar* indicating that R' Pinchas ben Yair was actually R' Shimon's father-in-law; based on this he considers emending the Talmudic text here.

3. The salt from the tears aggravated his wounds (*Rashi*).

The Talmud mentions R' Shimon's prowess in the revealed portion of Torah. As mentioned above, it was during his years in the cave that R' Shimon rose to the heights where the hidden realm of Torah became open before him. R' Shimon was certain that the physical deprivation to which he had been subjected, including the learning of Torah while buried up to his neck in sand, was a primary factor in his attainment of such awesome spiritual levels.

While we are far removed from such levels, there is a lesson to be learned nonetheless. The more one frees himself from earthly cravings and self-interest, the more he will succeed at spiritual accomplishment. And such freedom, writes *Nesivos Shalom,* is the key to happiness. A person whose life revolves around satisfying his own interests and urges will never be satisfied, while one whose goals and aspirations are Torah-oriented will find himself happy with his material lot and joyous with a life that is filled with meaning and accomplishment.[1]

The Zohar

⁂ At Sinai, the Oral and Written Laws in their entirety were transmitted to Moses. The totality of Torah study can be divided into four branches:

> פְּשַׁט, *the literal or evident meaning of the text;*
> רֶמֶז, *allegorical illustration of Scripture;*
> דְּרוּשׁ, *halachic and aggadic exegesis;*
> סוֹד, esoteric aspects of Torah [Kabbalah].

For generations, the esoteric portion of Torah was the province of a very few select *tzaddikim,* who transmitted these teachings privately and orally. After R' Shimon bar Yochai's emergence from the cave where he had attained awesome heights, he was granted Heavenly approval to form a חַבְרַיָּא קַדִּישָׁא, *Holy Fraternity,* a select

1. In this vein, *Nesivos Shalom* explains R' Shimon's declaration concerning the Romans: "Everything they established, they established only to serve their own needs." Knowing that the Romans were mired in self-indulgence, R' Shimon considered it impossible that their edifices could have been built with the Jews' interests in mind.

group of disciples to whom he would reveal secrets of the Torah.[1]

> And just as *Rabbeinu HaKadosh* [Rabbi Yehudah the Prince] did years later [with the endorsement of] all the Sages, to [record and] seal the Mishnah,[2] so too, did R' Shimon and his group establish a yeshivah to author an all-encompasing, awesome work of the Torah's secrets and [hidden] light (*R' Moshe Chaim Luzzato* in *Adir BaMarom*[3]).

Until that point, it had been God's will that these secrets remain hidden. With the onset of this long and difficult exile, however, revelation of these secrets became a necessity in order to effect the תִּיקוּנִים, *spiritual improvements,* which would help pave the way for the future redemption.[4] And while it is impossible for anyone to truly fathom the Torah's secrets "save when it is from the mouth of a wise *mekubal* [one versed in Kabbalah] to the ear of an understanding *mekubal,*"[5] nevertheless, Heaven sanc-

---

1. The greatest of these disciples was R' Shimon's son, R' Elazar, who is buried near him at the tomb in Meron.

2. Until that point, it had been forbidden to commit the Oral Law to writing, except for private notes which the teacher or student recorded for himself. Rabbi Yehudah the Prince compiled the Six Orders of the Mishnah as the fundamental book of the revealed portion of Oral Law because the times required it.

"He saw that the students were becoming fewer and fewer, and new calamities were constantly occurring. The Roman Empire was expanding throughout the world and gaining dominion, while the Jews were becoming more and more dispersed to even further corners of the earth. He therefore wrote [the Oral Law] into one book, so that everyone should be able to have access to it, so that they should [be able to] learn it quickly and it should not be forgotten (*Rambam,* Introduction to *Mishneh Torah*).

3. R' Moshe Chaim Luzzato, known as *Ramchal* (an acronym for רַבִּי מֹשֶׁה חַיִּים לוּצַטוֹ), was a renowned eighteenth-century kabbalist and ethicist. He authored many works, including the ethical classic *Mesilas Yesharim.* His *Adir BaMarom* is a kabbalistic commentary on the section of *Zohar* know as *Idra Rabba* (see p. 52).

4. *Ramchal,* ibid. See "A Light in the Darkness" which follows this section.

5. *Ramban* (preface to his commentary on the Torah). One should note that *Ramban* himself was one of those select few to whom the mystical traditions taught by R' Shimon bar Yochai were transmitted orally before they were published and disseminated. His commentary to the Torah is replete with kabbalistic interpretations, many of which are found in *Zohar.* The *Arizal* testified to the depth and reliability of the mystical portion of *Ramban's* commentary, and considered *Ramban* the last of the ancient kabbalistic school, who received direct transmission of the mystical secrets that were later concealed.

tioned the recording of these teachings, and at a later point in history, their publication and dissemination occurred.[1]

Thus did R' Shimon bar Yochai reveal the teachings which form the classic work of *Kabbalah, Sefer HaZohar* (the Book of Radiance),[2] also known as מִדְרָשׁ יְהִי אוֹר, *Midrash Let There be Light.* [3]

In addition to teaching his disciples that which was already known to the select few in every generation, R' Shimon attained understanding of and revealed teachings which had been communicated to Moses at Sinai but which had not been handed down from generation to generation.[4] Among the most esoteric teachings found in *Zohar* are the sections known as *Idra Rabba* [5] and *Idra Zuta.* [6] The latter was revealed by R' Shimon on the day on which he departed this world, the eighteenth of Iyar, Lag BaOmer.[7]

---

1. See *Toldos Am Olam,* vol. VI, p. 95.

2. The title *Sefer HaZohar* was granted Heavenly approval (preface to *Tikkunei Zohar*).

3. *Sefer Yuchsin* ch. 43. The words יְהִי אוֹר, *let there be light,* are from *Genesis* 1:3 and refer to the primeval light of Creation.

4. See 'A Spark of Moses' on p. 58.

5. Found in *Parashas Naso*. An *idra* is a circular *threshing floor* (see *Maharzu* to *Song of Songs* 7:11). Ostensibly, R' Shimon and his disciples sat in a circle when he revealed these teachings. Others define *idra* as a *gathering* (see *Bein Pesach L'Shavuos* p. 314.). *Rabba* and *zuta* mean *large* and *small* respectively, and indicate that when the *Idra Rabba* was revealed by R' Shimon, a larger group of disciples was present.

6. In *Parashas Haazinu.*

7. On the day on which he departed this world, R' Shimon instructed his disciple R' Abba to commit his esoteric teachings to writings (*Zohar* cited by *Bnei Yissoschor, Chodesh Iyar* 3:2). After its completion *Sefer HaZohar* was concealed, and for centuries, its teachings were handed down orally to the few in each generation who were among the יוֹדְעֵי חֵ"ן [חָכְמַת הַנִּסְתָּר], *those knowledgeable in hidden wisdom.*

R' Moshe de Leon (1250-1305), a kabbalist from Leon, Spain, earned his livelihood as a traveling scribe copying old manuscripts. It was he who discovered and published the *Zohar,* making its teachings available to the masses for the very first time. The publication caused great controversy, as some scholars contended that these teachings should remain the province of the select few.

R' Yitzchak D'Letash, a leading personality in that generation, issued a lengthy halachic ruling endorsing the *Zohar's* publication. (It is published in the standard edition of *Sefer HaZohar.*) In it he writes:

> . . . As our Sages taught: The first two thousand years, this world was empty [i.e. devoid of Torah], the second two thousand years were of Torah, the final two thousand are the days of the Messiah [i.e. the period which will lead to

R' Shimon Departs

ↄ In *Zohar* it is recorded[1] that on the day when R' Shimon bar Yochai was to depart this world, a spiritual fire surrounded his house.[2] R' Shimon rejoiced on that day and summoned his disciples, the *Chavraya Kadisha*.[3] R' Shimon said:

> The hour is a fortuitous one. I wish to enter the World to Come without shame.[4] Behold, there are sacred thoughts which I did not reveal until now. I wish to reveal them now before the Divine Presence . . .

R' Shimon then instructed his disciples individually. He told them that they had been joined on that day by the Divine Presence, accompanied by the souls of the righteous in Heaven. He said:

> *I am my Beloved's and His longing is upon me*[5] — All the days that I was bound to this world, I was [in fact] bound only to the Holy One, Blessed is He. Therefore, *His longing is upon me.*

R' Shimon then proceeded to reveal deep secrets of the Torah.

---

and ultimately result in the Messiah's arrival] (*Sanhedrin* 97a). In the first two thousand years, the world was not fit to receive the Torah, and during that time the Torah remained hidden in His treasure house. . .and only a select few — such as the Patriarchs and the Tribes — merited it. Then, the time came when the Torah was given at Mount Sinai in the presence of six hundred thousand.

And so it is with the secrets of the Torah, which until now were sealed, known only to a select few of spiritual striving, for the time had not yet come to disseminate them. However, in the two thousand years of the days of the Messiah, though due to our sins whatever has happened has happened [— probably a reference to the persecutions of that era], this branch of wisdom will become known and revealed to all . . .

1. As mentioned above, the *Zohar* was arranged and sealed by R' Shimon's disciples (*Sefer Yuchsin* and *Ramchal*), who included in it the account of R' Shimon's passing.

2. *Zohar, Parashas Haazinu.*

3. See p. 50.

4. I.e., R' Shimon wanted to fulfill what he knew to be the will of God, that he reveal the secrets which comprise the *Idra Zuta*.

5. *Song of Songs* 7:11.

In the course of his words R' Shimon said, "Until now, the words which I have revealed were concealed and hidden. . . It is known before the Ancient Holy One that not for my honor nor for my family's honor have I done this. . . Moreover, I have seen that the Holy One, Blessed is He, has approved of this, as well as the righteous [souls] who are present here. All of them are rejoicing with this joyous occasion of mine, and all of them are invited in That World to my joyous celebration. Praiseworthy is my lot!"

R' Shimon continued to reveal secrets of the Torah until he cited the verse, ". . .for there Hashem has commanded the blessing — may there be life forever!"[1] His disciple R' Abba related:

> The Holy Lamp [R' Shimon][2] had not completed the word חַיִּים, *life,* when his words were silenced. I had intended to continue to record [his teachings] but I heard nothing more. I did not lift up my head [to see what was transpiring] for the light was so great that I could not look. In the midst of this I was shaken when I heard a voice proclaiming, "For they add to you length of days and years of life and peace;"[3] and "Life he requested of You, You gave it to him; length of days forever and ever."[4]
>
> That entire day, the fire did not cease [from surrounding] the house and no one went near him [R' Shimon] for no one was able to approach him, for the light and fire surrounded him. . . When the fire departed, I saw that the holy luminary, holiest of holies, had departed this world. He was lying on his right side, enwrapped [in his *tallis*], a smile upon his countenance . . .[5]

As R' Shimon bar Yochai was being brought to Meron for burial, a Heavenly voice was heard: *"Assemble, come and gather for the* הִילוּלָא*, joyous celebration, of R' Shimon — 'He will come*

---

1. *Psalms* 133:3.

2. *Zohar* refers to R' Shimon as בּוּצִינָא קַדִּישָׁא, *Holy Lamp.* (*Targum Onkelos* translates נֵרֹתֶיהָ, her *lamps,* as בּוּצִינָהָא.) Some translate בּוּצִינָא קַדִּישָׁא as *holy spark,* for R' Shimon was a *nitzutz,* spark, of the soul of Moses (*Taamei HaMinhagim*).

3. *Proverbs* 3:2.

4. *Psalms* 21:5.

5. *Zohar, Parashas Haazinu.*

in peace, they will rest on their resting places.' "[1]

As the procession entered the cave in Meron where R' Shimon would be interred, a Heavenly voice proclaimed:

> *This is the man who made the land tremble, who made kingdoms quake!*[2] Many accusations in Heaven are being silenced today because of you! This is Rabbi Shimon bar Yochai, whose Master takes pride in him each day. Praiseworthy is his lot, Above and below. How many Heavenly storehouses are hidden away for him! Regarding him it is said, *As for you, go to your end; you will rest — then arise for your portion at the end of days.*[3]

King David beseeched his Creator: גַּל עֵינַי וְאַבִּיטָה נִפְלָאוֹת מִתּוֹרָתֶךָ, *Uncover my eyes that I may behold wonders of Your Torah.*[4] The word גַּל, *uncover,* can be reversed to read ל״ג, *Lag,* the intent being that on Lag BaOmer, the wonders of the hidden aspect of the Torah were revealed by Rabbi Shimon Bar Yochai. "On that day he ascended on High and instructed [his disciple] R' Abba to record the treasuries of esoteric teachings which he revealed, to leave us the blessing of the hidden light [of Creation], for ourselves and future generations until the light of the Messiah will be revealed, may it be speedily" *(Bnei Yissoschor).*

Thus, the celebration of Lag BaOmer commemorates the revelation of this portion of Torah, and is particularly appropriate in the days of *Sefirah* as we ready ourselves for the day on which all of Torah was given to Moses at Sinai.

---

1. *Isaiah* 57:2.

2. Ibid. 14:16.

3. *Daniel* 12:13. Also interred in the cave at Meron is R' Elazar, son of R' Shimon. The circumstances surrounding his interment are related in *Koheles Rabbah* 11:1. See also *Bava Metzia* 84b. He was interred on *erev* Yom Kippur.

Hilula D'Rashbi states: "Because of this, they perceive in Meron on *erev* Yom Kippur at the tomb of R' Elazar a great spiritual light. Apparently, each year on this day there is a renewal and reawakening of the gladness and spiritual aura when the exalted souls of father [R' Shimon] and son [R' Elazar] were reunited."

4. *Psalms* 119:18.

A Distinction

The day of a *yahrtzeit* (anniversary of a death) is generally a solemn day of fasting and prayer. For example, the seventh of Adar, the *yahrtzeit* of Moses, is listed among the days on which it is proper to fast.[1] There are those, therefore, who have questioned the passing of Rabbi Shimon on Lag BaOmer as a major cause of celebration.[2] However, as we have seen, it was on that day when R' Shimon revealed the *Idra Zuta* and instructed his disciple to record his teachings. This itself is cause for celebration. By contrast, during the thirty-day mourning period following Moses' death, three hundred laws were forgotten.[3] Therefore, celebration on that day is not in order (*Shaar Yissoschor*).

Moreover, as is apparent from the passages of *Zohar* cited above, R' Shimon himself rejoiced on the day of his death, and that day was referred to by the Heavenly voice as הִילוּלָא דְר׳ שִׁמְעוֹן, *the [day of] rejoicing of Rabbi Shimon.*

There is an additional reason for joy in that R' Shimon bar Yochai left behind a son, R' Elazar, who was his greatest disciple and a fitting successor to transmit his teachings (*Responsa Mayim Chaim*). As R' Shimon himself said:

> I have seen the people of the highest level [who receive the countenance of the Divine Presence] and they are few. If they are a thousand, I and my son are among them; if they are a hundred, I and my son are among them; if they are two, they are myself and my son (*Succah* 45b).

The Talmud defines the level of perception which R' Shimon and R' Elazar had attained as one of אַסְפַּקְלַרְיָא הַמְאִירָה, *[viewing the Shechinah through] a clear screen.* Moreover, they were permitted to approach the *Shechinah* without first asking permission of the angels who are appointed for this purpose.[4]

---

1. *Shulchan Aruch, Orach Chaim* 580:2.
2. See Responsa of *Chasam Sofer, Yoreh Deah* §233 and *Sho'el U'Meishiv* 5:39.
3. *Temurah* 16a.
4. The analogy is drawn to a royal household. Only the king's family members and those servants who attend to him at all times may enter his chamber without

R' Avraham HaLevi

In sixteenth-century Safed lived R' Avraham HaLevi, whose piety was extolled by the *Arizal*. Each night at midnight, R' Avraham would walk the streets of Safed and in a mournful voice would say, "Our brethren, the House of Israel: You are well aware that the *Shechinah* (Divine Presence) is in exile, due to our many sins, and our Temple has gone up in flames. Let us arise and cry out to God, Who is a merciful and compassionate King. Perhaps our prayers will be heeded and He will take pity on His nation, the remnants of Israel." The *Arizal* said that R' Avraham was a *gilgul* (transmigrant) of the prophet Jeremiah, the prophet of the First Destruction.[1]

It is a universal custom to recite the paragraph of נַחֵם (*Comfort*), mourning the Destruction of the Temple and supplicating that it be rebuilt, in the *Minchah Shemoneh Esrei* on the afternoon of Tishah B'Av. It was R' Avraham HaLevi's custom to recite this prayer throughout the year in every weekday *Shemoneh Esrei.* One year on Lag BaOmer, R' Avraham visited the tomb of R' Shimon, where he recited *Shemoneh Esrei* as usual. Upon completing it, the *Arizal* told him that the soul of R' Shimon bar Yochai had just appeared to him at the tomb and had strongly criticized R' Avraham for reciting this paragraph of mourning "on the day of our gladness."

The above was related by the *Arizal's* disciple R' Chaim Vital[2] who concluded the above account, "I have written all this to show that there is a strong source for the above-mentioned custom [to visit R' Shimon's tomb on Lag BaOmer and rejoice there]."

---

permission (*Eitz Yosef*).

Elsewhere, the Talmud states that only Moses perceived the Divine Presence as through a clear screen (*Yevamos* 49b). *Maharsha* differentiates between the attainment of this level through prophecy or through Torah. For other explanations, see *Aruch LaNer, Iyun Yaakov* and *Sfas Emes.*

1. See *Tishah B'Av: Texts, Readings and Insights* (ArtScroll Holiday Series), pp. 84-85.

2. *Shaar HaKavanos* p. 87b. See *Ba'er Heiteiv* to *Shulchan Aruch, Orach Chaim* 493:4.

In the Talmud, the term הִילּוּלָא, *hilula,* refers to a wedding celebration.[1] In Kabbalah, the passing of a *tzaddik,* who ascends to the highest heavens, is likened to a marriage. Moreover, a Jew's existence on this world, where he studies the revealed portion of Torah, is likened to a betrothal [אֵירוּסִין], while his existence in the Next World, where the secrets of the Torah are revealed to him, is likened to the completion of the marriage process [נִשּׂוּאִין]. The day of Rabbi Shimon's passing, when he revealed the secrets of the Torah, had an aura of spiritual joy akin to that of the Next World, and thus is a day of celebration (*HaMoadim BeHalachah*).

The sixteenth-century Kabbalist R' Avraham Galante writes[2] that on the day of a *tzaddik's* death, the merits of the good deeds and Torah study of his entire life are reawakened and come together to impact in the Upper Realms in a profound way. This, he writes, is the "secret" of the *hilula* of R' Shimon bar Yochai.

Midrash Rus records that when R' Chisdai died, his son R' Yosei spent the night in the cemetery listening to the rejoicing of legions of angels who said, "Let us go to the joyous celebration of the Torah of R' Chisdai."[3]

A Spark of Moses

The writings of the *Arizal* and *Ramchal,* as well as the commentary *Mikdash Melech* to *Zohar,* state that the soul of R' Shimon bar Yochai was a *nitzutz,* spark, of the soul of Moses.[4]

---

1. See, for example, *Berachos* 6b.

2. In *Kinas Sesarim.* R' Galante was a disciple of the famed kabbalist R' Moshe Cordovero.

3. In chassidic circles, a *tzaddik's yahrtzeit* is customarily celebrated with a *seudas mitzvah* (*mitzvah* banquet) and rejoicing.

4. The name לַ״ג בָּעוֹמֶר would seem to be accurate only according to *Nusach Ashkenaz,* in which the text of the nightly *Sefirah* counting reads: הַיּוֹם . . . שֶׁהֵם . . . בָּעוֹמֶר. According to *Nusach Sefard,* however, where the text reads, הַיּוֹם . . . שֶׁהֵם . . . לָעוֹמֶר, the day should be known as לַ״ג לָעוֹמֶר. The *Maggid* of Trisk (cited by *Taamei HaMinhagim*) noted that לַ״ג בָּעֹמֶר (in the diminutive spelling) is numerically equal

In *Hilula D'Rashbi,* R' Asher Zelig Margulies draws no less than *sixty* parallels between Moses and R' Shimon. For example: Moses fled Egypt when Pharaoh sought to kill him[1] and during his years as a fugitive, as a shepherd in the wilderness, he attained his *shleimus,* spiritual perfection. R' Shimon fled when the Romans sought to kill him and it was during his years in the cave that he attained his *shleimus.*

Parallel Fifteen reads:

> Moses received the Torah at Sinai. Regarding R' Shimon bar Yochai it is stated: "From the day that R' Shimon left the cave. . . sublime secrets were shown and revealed [while he was] with his disciples, as if they were given at that moment at Sinai."[2]
>
> R' Shimon himself declared: "I have been shown now that which no man has seen from the day that Moses ascended Mount Sinai a second time."[3]
>
> Our master the *Arizal* states: "At the time when [he revealed] the *Idra Rabba,* R' Shimon bar Yochai, of blessed memory, ascended to the level which our teacher Moses, of blessed memory, attained when he received the Second Tablets — but he did not attain the level of Moses when he received the First Tablets."[4]
>
> With this, we can understand the statement [regarding the *Idra Rabba*]: "When R' Shimon bar Yochai began

---

to מֹשֶׁה (345), alluding to the relationship between Moses and R' Shimon bar Yochai.

According to the *Arizal's* order of the *Ushpizin,* Exalted Guests of Succos, Moses leads the *Ushpizin* on the festival's fourth day. Lag BaOmer always falls on the same weekday as the fourth day of the following Succos holiday.

רַעְיָא מְהֵימְנָא, *Faithful Shepherd,* is the appellation accorded Moses in the writings of *Kabbalah.* R' Shimon bar Yochai authored a mystical exposition on the Torah's commandments entitled רַעְיָא מְהֵימְנָא. (It is published togther with *Sefer HaZohar* which is arranged according to the *Sidrahs* of the Torah.) The secrets contained in רַעְיָא מְהֵימְנָא were revealed when the soul of Moses became garbed in R' Shimon's body (R' Moshe Chaim Luzzato in *Adir BaMarom*).

1. *Exodus* 2:15.
2. *Zohar,* standard edition, Vol. I, p. 216b.
3. *Zohar,* Vol. III, p. 132b.
4. *Shaar HaGilgulim* ch. 36, p. 47b (by the *Arizal's* disciple R' Chaim Vital) and *Shaar Maamarei Rashbi* 44b.

[revealing] the secrets of secrets, the ground shook"[1] which is explained [in *Ruach David*]: "The place shook, resembling what took place at Sinai. . ."

Based on the above, *Sefer Hilula D'Rashbi* draws another distinction between the seventh of Adar, the yahrtzeit of Moses, and Lag BaOmer, the yahrtzeit of R' Shimon bar Yochai. Moses was not permitted to enter the Land Of Israel, though he offered copious prayers that he be granted this privilege.[2] This is why his yahrtzeit is a solemn day. On Lag BaOmer we rejoice that R' Shimon, a nitzutz (spark) of Moses, was granted burial in the Holy Land.

R' Asher Zelig Margulies, who himself was a revered *tzaddik* and kabbalist, writes that it was an age-old custom among the kabbalists of Safed, and in later generations among the pious of Jerusalem as well, to visit the tomb of R' Shimon on the seventh of Adar. "In truth, one can perceive there on the seventh of Adar a perception of the great light of the gladness of Moses, who rejoices over his portion which found expression in the person of R' Shimon bar Yochai" *(Hilula D'Rashbi).*

A Heavenly Debate

The Talmud[3] relates that when Moses ascended to Heaven to receive the Torah, the angels contended that the Torah was too sublime to be given to men of flesh and blood. God instructed Moses, "Respond to them." Moses, however, was frightened, "I fear [to reply] lest they burn me with the breath in their mouths." God said to him, "Take hold of the Throne of My Glory and give them an answer."

Moses then presented a convincing argument proving that the Torah was intended for man, not angels. ". . . Do you [angels] engage in labor from which you need to rest [on the Sabbath]? . . . Are there any business transactions among you [that might lead

1. *Idra Rabba* 128a.
2. See *Deuteronomy* 3:23-27.
3. *Shabbos* 88b-89a.

you to transgress the law against false oaths]? . . .Do you have a father and mother [to honor]?" The Talmudic account concludes, "Immediately, every one of the angels became a friend of Moses and gave him something, as it is written,[1] 'You ascended to the heights, you captured a captive, you took gifts because of man.' "

Maharsha explains that the angels' contention was only that the hidden portion of Torah, which relates to matters which are purely spiritual, belonged in the Heavens among beings who are purely spiritual. God's response to Moses, "Take hold of the Throne of My Glory. . ." meant that a *tzaddik,* through his attachment to God, can also comprehend such knowledge. Moses' argument then prevailed. ". . .Do you [angels] engage in labor from which you need to rest [on the Sabbath]? . . ." The revealed portion of Torah was clearly intended for man, and therefore man should be given the hidden portion of Torah as well. The angels were convinced and they presented Moses with gifts — knowledge of the hidden portion of Torah.

Ramchal notes that the word שֶׁבִי, *captive,* is an acronym for שִׁמְעוֹן בַּר יוֹחַאי, the implication being that some of the "gifts" revealed to Moses at that time would not be revealed to any other man until the spark of Moses that was R' Shimon bar Yochai was granted Heavenly consent to reveal them.

The Aura Remains

⇐§ The *Arizal* taught that on the day when an exalted soul prepares to depart this world, the totality of *mitzvos* which he performed during his lifetime and the Torah which he studied come together and shine with a brilliant light. The moment is an עֵת רָצוֹן, a most auspicious time for spiritual attainment and for one's aspirations to be fulfilled. It was with the radiance of such light that R' Shimon bar Yochai, whose self-sacrifice for the sake of Torah is beyond comprehension, was able to reveal the awesome סודות, *secrets,* of the Torah which he bequeathed to his disciples on the last day of his life.

---

1. *Psalms* 68:19.

R' Moshe Teitelbaum, author of *Yismach Moshe,* is quoted[1] as saying: "Though almost two thousand years have elapsed since the day on which R' Shimon bar Yochai departed this world, the spiritual aura of that awesome day still descends to this world each year on his *yahrtzeit.* Every Jew, according to his spiritual level, can perceive this aura on Lag BaOmer, a day that remains an עֵת רָצוֹן for all generations."

A Light in the Darkness

With this work, the Sefer HaZohar, it [the Jewish Nation] will be redeemed from exile (Zohar, Parashas Naso).

A Prediction and A Promise

The Talmud[2] relates:

When our Rabbis entered the Vineyard in Yavneh[3], they said, "The Torah will eventually be forgotten from [the Nation of] Israel, as it is written, *Behold, days are coming, declares* HASHEM, *when I will send a hunger into the land; not a hunger for bread and not a thirst for water, but to hear the word of* HASHEM.[4] And it is written [in the verse that follows which describes the search that will ensue], *And they shall journey from sea to sea and from the north unto the east, they shall wander to seek the word of* HASHEM *but shall not find it.*

. . . R' Shimon ben Yochai said: Heaven forfend that the Torah would be forgotten from Israel! For it is written, *For it shall not be forgotten from the mouth of [the nation's] offspring.*[5]

---

1. In *Doresh Tov* by R' Nachum Mordechai of Chortkov.

2. *Shabbos* 138b.

3. Yavneh was for a time the seat of the *Sanhedrin* (Supreme Court) where the Torah scholars were arranged in rows [according to their level of scholarship] much as the grapevines of a vineyard are arranged.

4. *Amos* 8:11,12.

5. R' Shimon goes on to offer a different interpretation of Amos' prophecy. The Sages would interpret the verse cited by R' Shimon as a promise that the historical prophecies contained in *Shiras Haazinu* (*Deuteronomy* 32:1-43) would never become forgotten (*Maharsha*).

It would appear that R' Shimon and the Sages argued about the severity of the exile and whether or not it could actually cause Torah to become "forgotten."[1] This, says R' Yaakov Meir Schechter of Jerusalem (*V'Nichtav BaSefer*), is not the case. Scripture and the writings of our Sages make clear that the fourth and final exile, in particular, will be awesome in its potential for domination and spiritual catastrophe: " . . . a fourth beast, excessively terrifying, awesome and strong; with immense iron teeth, it was eating and crumbling, and trampling the rest with its feet; it was different from all the beasts that preceded it . . .[2]

The Sages foresaw, with their spiritual vision, the sufferings, persecutions, destructions and foreign influences with which the Jewish people would be plagued during this exile. And they concluded that according to the natural order, the Torah would ultimately become forgotten.

R' Shimon did not dispute this. He arrived at his opinion by looking beyond the natural order, as R' Shechter explains by way of a parable.

The Rescuer

A crowd watched in horror as a child fell from a rooftop. It appeared that the child was headed to his death. Someone in the crowd yelled, "He's going to live!" This man, of exceptional swiftness, agility and strength, dashed forward and snatched the child out of the air as he hurtled toward the ground.

The child represents the Children of Israel in exile and the man who saved them is R' Shimon bar Yochai.

On the day of his death, R' Shimon bar Yochai declared, "All the days that I was bound to this world, I was [in fact] bound only to the Holy One, Blessed is He."[3] His attachment to God was through his awesome level of Torah study. *Zohar* states that when R' Shimon would study Torah, the Heavenly angels would fall

---

1. The Sages explain this to mean that there will come a time when there will be no one who possesses knowledge of *Halachah*.

2. *Daniel* 7:7. See also *Bereishis Rabbah* 2:4.

3. See p. 53.

silent as all turned their attention to the wisdom which flowed from his lips.[1]

Through his *Sefer HaZohar,* he bequeathed to all future generations a spiritual light from which a Jew can draw strength to persevere in the most difficult situations. Moreover, in bequeathing the סודות, *secrets,* of the Torah, to future generations, R' Shimon also bequeathed an approach to life which encourages a Jew to "look beneath the surface." Just as R' Shimon demonstrates in *Sefer HaZohar* how in the hidden realm, the *Tochachah,* Admonition, is actually a blessing in disguise,[2] so too, is it possible to accept even the darkest situation as an expression of God's goodness, and in so doing maintain one's faith, devotion to His teachings and joy in His service at all times (*R' Moshe Wolfson*).

R' Shimon perceived all this and thus did he declare with confidence: "Heaven forfend that the Torah would be forgotten from Israel! For it is written, כִּי לֹא תִשָּׁכַח מִפִּי זַרְעוֹ *For it shall not be forgotten from the mouth of [the nation's] offspring.*" The final letters of the words כִּי לֹא תִשָּׁכַח מִפִּי זַרְעוֹ, when rearranged, form the name יוֹחָאי, *Yochai.* It was through R' Shimon, the זֶרַע, *offspring,* of Yochai, that the continuity of Torah life was ensured (*R' Nachman of Breslov*).

Serve God with Gladness

King David said: "Serve HASHEM with gladness, come before Him with joyous song."[3] Especially in Chassidic thought, the quality of *simchah,* gladness, is considered fundamental for proper service of God.

Nesivos Shalom[4] defines the "source" of such joy:

> A Jew rejoices in the way in which God acts towards him. The source of this joy is a deep-rooted feeling that God is a trustworthy, merciful Father Who is devoted to him, and Who is constantly watching over him in order to benefit

1. *Zohar, Parashas Shemos.*
2. See p. 128.
3. *Psalms* 100:2.
4. Vol. I, p. 286.

him . . . Whether or not he understands and perceives the benefit, he is permeated with a pure faith that "whatever the Merciful One does is for the good."

The quality of *gladness* is an exalted one; *Toras Avos* states that when a Jew accepts God's conduct towards him with gladness, then measure for measure, God accepts his service with gladness, even when it is somewhat lacking.

Through such clarity of vision, a Jew perceives even in times of travail that "I [God] am with him in distress."[1] And regardless of what will occur, even when he experiences a downward turn in his level of service, he will perceive a closeness with God, that God is with him even while his soul is experiencing distress and that he is not alone — a feeling that "Though I walk in the valley of death, I will fear no evil for You are with me."[2]

Through this feeling that God is always with him, and that "He alone made, makes and will make everything,"[3] one is in a constant state of gladness.

The idea that God's love for every Jew is unconditional, that even when a Jew stumbles spiritually, God is always at his side, ready to extend a hand, as it were, is also an outgrowth of the teachings of *Zohar* and is a fundamental of Chassidic thought. This idea, too, has saved many a soul in exile from hopelessness and despair and is yet another reason why it was R' Shimon who declared that, come what may, the Torah would never become forgotten.

An Awesome, Sanctifed Day

The day of the hilula (joyous celebration) of R' Shimon bar Yochai has a unique status, the likes of which is not found by other tzaddikim . . . the people of Israel, if they are

1. *Psalms* 91:15.
2. Ibid. 23:4.
3. The first of the *Rambam's* Thirteen Principles of Faith.

not prophets, they are descendants of prophets;[1] *it is their desire to attach themselves to the light of Rashbi (Nesivos Shalom).*

A Time for Salvation

☙ In a halachic discussion related to the laws of Shabbos, the Talmud concludes that, "R' Shimon [bar Yochai] is [sufficiently] worthy to be relied upon in a time of emergency" (*Shabbos* 45a). Interpreting this homiletically, *Sefer Kol Aryeh* writes:

> R' Shimon Bar Yochai's merits are great, and in his merit, one can arouse [the Attribute of] Mercy before our Father in Heaven. One can also arouse the *tzaddik* [R' Shimon, in his place in *Gan Eden*], so that utilizing his merits, he will seek mercy before our Father in Heaven that we should be rescued from our travails and distress. *R' Shimon [bar Yochai] is [sufficiently] worthy to be relied upon in a time of emergency* — in a period such as we are now experiencing when we are distressed and afflicted.[2]

A Time for Prayer

☙ The day of Lag BaOmer is auspicious for healing of the soul and the spirit (*Orah V'Simchah* p. 20).

The great eighteenth-century scholar R' Yonasan Eibeschutz wrote:

---

1. See *Pesachim* 66a.

2. R' Yekusiel Yehudah Halberstam, the late Klausenberger *Rebbe,* related that the spiritual efforts on Lag BaOmer of the Chassidic master R' Moshe of Rozvidov (great-grandson of R' Naftoli of Ropshitz) were unlike anything seen in his court the rest of the year. On that day, men, women and children would come before the *Rebbe* to receive his blessing. His countenance on that day reflected the intensity of the Days of Awe.

One year as Lag BaOmer drew to a close, R' Moshe said, "הַשֶּׁמֶשׁ יָבֹא וְיִפְנֶה (*The sun will set and be gone* — from the Yom Kippur *Neilah* service) —Oh! If only the sun could stay put for a while so that we could enjoy the sanctity of this day a bit longer!"

> The day of Lag BaOmer is the *hilula* of R' Shimon bar Yochai. He died on that day and in Heaven there was joyous celebration . . . It is fitting for everyone who possesses awe of God in his heart to repent on that day, for the merit of R' Shimon bar Yochai will assist those who come to purify themselves. [And certainly] one should not waste his day with vanities of the world . . .

A number of medieval commentators wrote that this day is auspicious for being granted the blessing of children. Some advise the couple to vow that if a son will be born to them, he will be named "Shimon" after R' Shimon bar Yochai, or that the child's *upsherin* (first haircut) will take place in Meron at the tomb of R' Shimon. There are other *segulos* (auspicious omens) related to this as well.[1]

The letters of מֵרוֹן, *Meron,* are an acronym for מֶלֶךְ רוֹפֵא נֶאֱמָן וְרַחֲמָן, *the King, Who is a faithful and compassionate healer,* a hint to the healing powers of Lag BaOmer in merit of R' Shimon bar Yochai who is buried in Meron (*Hilula D'Rashbi* citing *Lechem Shlomo*). Therefore, one should pray on this day with added intensity that the sick be cured of their illnesses and that the barren be granted children.

As mentioned above, it was on the eighteenth of Iyar, the day on which Lag BaOmer falls, that the manna began to fall from Heaven during the Jews' sojourn in the Wilderness. It was then that a flow of spiritual and material blessing was initiated, for that generation and for their posterity. Every year on Lag BaOmer, this aura of blessing is manifest, making the day a most auspicious

---

1. In his work *Tal Yerushalayim,* R' Yehudah Leib Orenstein wrote:

"When I was in Meron on Lag BaOmer for the *hilula* of R' Shimon, I met two men who were distributing wine and liquor to everyone. I asked them why they were doing this. One of them replied that he had been childless after fourteen years of marriage. Then, on Lag BaOmer at Meron, he announced, 'I hereby donate eighteen *roytel* (approximately 53 liters) of wine in honor of *Rashbi's* celebration, so that *Hashem* will help me to have a son this year.' The entire assemblage reponded, *'Amen!'* His friend, who had been childless after ten years of marriage called out, 'And I donate the same!' That year both their wives gave birth to sons. This year, they had come to Meron to celebrate their sons' first haircuts and to fulfill their vows.

"I heard this from them myself."

See "Lag BaOmer Stories" in this volume for a recent episode involving this *segulah.*

time to pray that one be granted needs of both body and spirit (*R' Yaakov of Huseyatin*).

Of Time and Place

Great Chassidic masters[1] would say that one's service of God on Lag BaOmer can accomplish that which can be achieved on Yom Kippur. This requires explanation.[2]

In the spiritual realm, there are similar concepts of holiness which find expression in *makom,* place; *zman,* time; and *nefesh,* soul. One example of this is the Sabbath, Jerusalem and the *Kohen.* The Sabbath is the *time* which is sanctified as a day apart from the rest of the week; the sanctity of the holy city of Jerusalem is above that of the other cities in Israel;[3] and the sanctity of the *Kohen* sets him apart from his fellow Jews.[4]

This idea finds expression in yet a higher form. The *Kodesh HaKadashim,* Holy of Holies, the abode of the Divine Presence, was beyond the limits of nature. The Talmud teaches that the space taken up by the Ark in the Holy of Holies is not included in the room's dimensions, for miraculously it did not take up any space.[5] Yet this miracle is not listed among the miracles which occurred regularly in the First Temple.[6] The *Kodesh HaKadashim* was a place which, in a very literal sense, belonged to another world and therefore was, by its very essence, above the plane of nature.

Yom Kippur is the *Kodesh HaKadashim's* counterpart in *time.* It is called שַׁבַּת שַׁבָּתוֹן, *Sabbath of Sabbaths,* the most sanctified day

1. Among them, R' Shalom of Belz and his son R' Yehoshua; and R' Yehoshua of Kamarna as quoted in *Sefer Nitei Gavriel.*

2. What follows is based on a taped discourse of R' Moshe Wolfson, and his writings in *Emunas Itecha.*

3. *Mishnah Keilim* 1:8.

4. It allows him the exclusive privilege of performing the Temple service and requires that, even today, he avoid defilement and that he be accorded honor. See *Leviticus* 21:1-8.

5. *Megillah* 10b. When one would measure the width of the Holy of Holies, he would find that the space between the Ark and the side walls accounted for the room's entire width, for the Ark itself took up no space.

6. *Avos* 5:7.

of the year. It is a a day on which the Jewish people are lifted beyond earthly existence, to the level of angels who neither eat nor drink. When the Temple stood, it was only on Yom Kippur that the *Kohen Gadol,* the day's counterpart in *soul,* was permitted to enter the Holy of Holies, a place that is beyond this world.

In the Torah's agricultural cycle for the Land of Israel, every seventh year for seven cycles is sanctified as *Shemittah,* when the land must lie fallow. *Yovel,* the climactic fiftieth year, has yet a higher sanctity. In addition to the laws governing *Shemittah, Yovel* is a time when all Jewish slaves must go free and when all properties sold in Israel during the previous forty-nine years must return to their original owners. In Jewish thought, the number seven represents nature while eight is beyond the plane of nature.[1] In a deeper sense, *Yovel,* the year beyond the seven cycles of seven years, is an other-worldly year, when the stains of the soul are hidden by a Heavenly light which reveals the essential greatness of every Jewish soul. It is a time when every Jew reconnects with his Heavenly source, when he can begin anew. The Torah's laws regarding *Yovel* allude to this concept. *It is a Yovel year for you, and you shall return, each man to his ancestral heritage, each man to his family* (*Leviticus* 25:10).

The *shofar* blast at the conclusion of Yom Kippur recalls the *shofar* of *Yovel,*[2] because Yom Kippur and *Yovel* embody similar concepts. On Yom Kippur the Accuser is silenced, for every Jew is akin to an angel as he "returns to his source" and his essential sanctity is revealed.

Hidden within the day of Lag BaOmer, a weekday holiday of Rabbinic origin, is a semblance of these spiritual elements.

A Sabbath Soul

As already mentioned, Lag BaOmer is the day of הוֹד שֶׁבְּהוֹד, *glory within glory.* Rabbi Akiva taught that the word הוֹד alludes to the

1. The number seven symbolizes the complete purpose of human existence, combining the spiritual level of the Sabbath with the physical effort of the week. Going beyond seven, the number eight symbolizes man's abilities to transcend the limitations of physical existence *(Maharal).*

2. According to *R' Hai Gaon.* See ArtScroll *Yom Kippur Machzor.*

Holy Temple.[1] It follows, then, that the Holy of Holies was הוד שֶׁבְּהוד. Thus, Lag BaOmer, too, is a day whose essence is beyond the realm of nature, a day on which the essential greatness of every Jewish soul is revealed.

R' Shimon bar Yochai is described in *Zohar* as שַׁבְּתָא דְכוּלָא שַׁתָא, *Sabbath of the entire year.* In *Zohar,* Elijah the Prophet refers to R' Shimon as "Sabbath" and R' Yehudah says, "Just as the Sabbath is sanctified unto God, so too, is R' Shimon bar Yochai . . . "[2]

R' Shimon, through his sublime service of God, especially during his thirteen years in the cave with his son, was not bound by the natural order. For him, every day was akin to the Sabbath, a day of the soul. Moreover, he lived in a realm which was akin to the *day of everlasting Sabbath* of the World to Come. [3]

The famous *zemer, Bar Yochai,* which is universally sung on Lag BaOmer, is replete with kabbalistic ideas. While these are beyond us, a number of the terms used refer to the *time-place-soul* equation discussed above:

> *Bar Yochai! — in the Holy of Holies . . .*
> *Seven weeks are the secret of fifty . . .*
> *Fortunate are those who can plumb your mystery,*
> *garbed in the priestly breastplate . . .*

R' Shimon bar Yochai embodied the other-worldly concept of *Yovel.* He perceived the essential greatness of every Jew every day of the year, for he lived in a higher realm.

As mentioned above, the 600,000 letters of the Torah correspond to the souls of the Jewish people.[4] Just as every word of the Torah can be expounded upon through the methods of פַּרְדֵס [פְּשַׁט, רֶמֶז, דְרוּשׁ, סוֹד],[5] so, too, there are many layers to the soul of a Jew — from פְּשַׁט, the apparent spiritual standing of the

---

1. *Berachos* 58a.

2. *Zohar,* vol. III, pp. 144-145. The *gematria* of שִׁמְעוֹן בַּר יוֹחַאי equals 703, and that of שַׁבָּת is 702 (*Sefer Shir Bar Yochai*). In the discipline of *gematria,* a difference of 1 is not significant (*Bnei Yissoschor;* see *Sabbath:Its Essence and Significance,* p. 67).

3. Remarkably, with regard to the laws of Sabbath, the Talmud states (*Shabbos* 157a) that the *halachah,* with few exceptions, follows the opinion of R' Shimon.

4. See p. 39.

5. See p. 50

individual, to his סוד, the *secret* of his spiritual essence. Just as R' Shimon bar Yochai revealed the סודות, *secrets,* hidden in the Torah, so too did he reveal the secret of every Jewish soul.

The day of his *hilula* (joyous celebration), on which he revealed deep secrets of the Torah, is one of spiritual upliftment and invests our prayers and *mitzvos* with added potency. In this sense, Lag BaOmer is akin to the Days of Awe.

A Kingdom of Kohanim

It is noteworthy that in *Tractate Shabbos,* it was R' Shimon who ruled that "All Jews are sons of kings" (*Shabbos* 67a), which, in its plain meaning, has halachic ramifications. In a deeper sense, R' Shimon is alluding to Israel's status as a "kingdom of *Kohanim* and a holy nation"[1] which they attained at Sinai.

Rambam concludes the laws of *Shemittah* and *Yovel* with the following:

> Why did the [tribe of] Levi not receive a portion of the Land of Israel and its spoils along with his fellow Jews? Because he was separated to serve God, to attend to His service and to teach His upright ways and righteous laws to the multitudes, as it is written: *They shall teach Your ordinances to Jacob and Your Torah to Israel.*[2] Therefore, they are separated from the ways of the world; they do not join in battle like the rest of Israel, they do not inherit the Land, and they do not acquire for themselves through their physical strength. Rather, they are God's legion, as it is written, *Bless,* HASHEM, *His legion . . .*[3] And He, Blessed is He, acquires for them, as it is written, *I am your share and your heritage . . .*[4]
>
> *And [this applies] not to the tribe of Levi alone.* Rather,

1. *Exodus* 19:6.
2. *Deuteronomy* 33:10.
3. Ibid. v. 11.
4. *Numbers* 18:20.

> each and every man who has come into this world, if his spirit will inspire him and if his intellect will give him understanding, has the opportunity to separate himself, to stand before God to attend and serve Him. If he will truly understand God and follow the straight path and remain as God has originally made Him; if he will cast off his neck the burden of the many contrivances and calculations which men seek out, then, indeed, this man will be truly sacred, a holy of holies, and God will be His estate forever and for all eternity. In this world, he will be allotted an amount which will suffice for his needs just as God has provided amply for the *Kohanim* and *Leviim*. This is as David, of blessed memory, said,[1] "HASHEM is my share, You guide my destiny" (*Hilchos Shemittah V'Yovel* 13:13).

It was R' Shimon bar Yochai who declared:

> If a man plows at the time of plowing, and sows at the time of sowing, and harvests at the time of harvesting, and threshes at the time of threshing, and winnows at the time of winnowing — what will become of the study of Torah?! Rather, at the time when the Jewish people do the will of the Omnipresent, their work is done for them by others (*Berachos* 35b).

R' Shimon was, as explained above, a "Sabbath soul" to whom every day, like Sabbath, was invested with an other-worldly aura. Thus, to R' Shimon, every day was to be devoted entirely to spiritual pursuits. Lag BaOmer contains within it an other-worldy aura to which every Jew can attach himself. It is a day on which a Jew can attain that which might otherwise be beyond his spiritual reach, a day when every Jew should rededicate himself to spiritual pursuits with renewed vigor and joy.

The Purim Connection

Shulchan Aruch (428:1) makes note of the fact that Purim and Lag BaOmer always fall on the same day of the week, indicating a

1. *Psalms* 16:5.

connection between the two. Both are weekdays, and both are holidays of intense joy. Both allude to the essential holiness of even the simple "weekday" Jew and both are days when every Jew can ignite this spark of holiness anew.

The Talmud states that the decree of annihilation which preceded the Purim miracle came about because the Jews particpated in the feast of King Ahasuerus.[1] *Chasam Sofer* notes that events which took place at that very feast actually paved the way for the Jews' salvation. Queen Vashti angered the king, was sentenced to death and Esther was appointed her successor. How could the very feast which aroused Heavenly judgment towards the Jews bring about their miraculous rescue?! The answer to this is that when a Jew sins, his essential holiness is not lost and he is still beloved in the eyes of God. "As a man will chastise his son, HASHEM, your God, chastises you" (*Deuteronomy* 8:5). Because the Jews had sinned, God deemed it necessary to bring about their repentance through Haman's decree, but in His infinite mercy and love of His people, He already set in motion the chain of events which led to their salvation. Thus, Purim and Lag BaOmer both point to the Jew's indestructible spiritual core.[2]

Above, we showed a parallel between Lag BaOmer and Yom Kippur. *Tikkunei Zohar* equates Purim and Yom Kippur.[3] *Sfas*

---

1. *Megillah* 12a.

2. *Shulchan Aruch* (428:1) offers the word פְּלַ״ג as an acronym for פּוּרִים – לַ״ג [בָּעוֹמֶר]. The word פְּלַג indicates a *division* or *break-off* (as in פְּלַג הַמִּנְחָה). This alludes to the association of both these holidays with even the lowest souls, who have "broken off' from the sacred ways and traditions of Torah life. Even they can draw new spirit from the aura of Purim and Lag BaOmer and find their way back to their roots.

There is a system of *gematria* (numerical equivalents) in which one counts the numerical total of all the letters used in pronouncing a given word. (Example: The letter ו equals 6, but when written the way it is pronounced [וָו, *vav*] it equals 12.) When calculating the *gematria* of מֵירוֹן , the site of R' Shimon Bar Yochai's tomb, in this way [מֵם, יוּד, רֵישׁ, וָו, נוּן] we arrive at a total of 738, the same as הַקְּרוֹבִים וְהָרְחוֹקִים, *the near and the far* (*Esther* 9:20) — the totality of Israel, whose collective soul is ignited by the spirit of Purim and Lag BaOmer (*R' Moshe Wolfson*).

The word פּוּרִים has the same *gematria* as אַהֲרֹן הַכֹּהֵן (336). As mentioned (see p. 33), Aaron represented the *Sefirah*/Emanation of הוֹד, *glory,* and Lag BaOmer is the day of הוֹד שֶׁבְּהוֹד (*R' Avraham S. Horowitz* in *Orah V'Simchah*).

3. In its literal sense, יוֹם הַכִּפּוּרִים, *Yom HaKippurim,* means *Day of Atonement. Tikkunei Zohar* interprets this title homiletically: יוֹם כְּפּוּרִים, *A Day Like Purim.*

Emes notes that with both of these festivals, the breaching of barriers plays a role. On Yom Kippur, the *Kohen Gadol* entered the Holy of Holies; on Purim, Esther entered Ahasuerus' inner sanctum.[1] This outward similarity indicates that on both these days, formidable spiritual barriers are breached. Spiritual goals which may be unattainable all year long may be attained on these festivals.

In *Song of Songs,* Israel declares: *I am black with sin, but beautiful nonetheless (Song of Songs* 1:5). *Midrash* interprets this as referring to Yom Kippur. Though Israel may appear to be besmirched by sin, this is only on the surface. Every Yom Kippur this facade gives way to our true nature, the inner beauty of the Jewish people. The same is true of Purim and Lag BaOmer.

A Day of Love and Divine Mercy

In the writings of Kabbalah, the days of *Sefirah* are seen as a time of Heavenly judgment.[2] Lag BaOmer, however, is viewed as a day flowing with Heavenly love and mercy.

Above, we discussed the *Sefiros*/Emanations and how they relate to the *Sefirah*/Counting period. Lag BaOmer is the day of הוֹד שֶׁבְּהוֹד, *glory within glory.* The word הוד is related to הוֹדָאָה, *praise* or *thanks.* The Torah tells us that Leah named her fourth son יְהוּדָה because הַפַּעַם אוֹדֶה אֶת ה׳, *"This time let me gratefully praise* HASHEM.*"*[3] It was R' Shimon bar Yochai who taught, "From the day the Holy One, Blessed is He, created His world, no man praised Him until Leah came and praised Him."[4] As *Rashi* (based on *Midrash*) explains, Leah was thanking God for giving her more than her share of sons, for she knew that Jacob was destined to have four wives and twelve sons. Thus, while others who preceded Leah expressed their praise of God, she was the first to declare that God had bestowed upon her something to which she was not entitled and was not in need of.[5]

Judgment means that one receives exactly what he deserves,

1. See *Esther* ch. 5.
2. See footnote on p. 34.
3. *Bereishis* 29:35.
4. *Berachos* 7b.
5. *Sefer Sifsei Chachamim* ad loc. citing *Maggid Ta'alumah.*

whether for good or for the opposite. The concept of הוֹד is that one is given more than he deserves. Moreover, as mentioned above, on Lag BaOmer, the essential, indestructible spiritual core of every Jewish soul is revealed. Thus, on this day of הוֹד שֶׁבְּהוֹד, the judgment of *Sefirah* is superseded by a Divine flow of blessing and compassion for even the lowliest soul.

Freeing the World from Judgment

As the Talmud relates,[1] upon emerging from the cave after twelve years there, R' Shimon and his son were distressed to find people tending to their material needs. They returned to the cave for another year, until a Heavenly voice proclaimed, "Emerge from your cave!" It was then that R' Shimon had attained a level where, from his exalted vantage point, he could perceive the good in every Jew and experience a feeling of true love for him.

R' Shimon once declared:

> I am able to exempt the entire world from judgment from the day that I was born until now. And were my son, Elazar, with me, [we could exempt the world] from the day the world was created until now. And were Yosam the son of Uziyahu [King of Judah] with us, from the day the world was created until its end.[2]

A *tzaddik* such as R' Shimon, who loved every Jew, had within his power, measure for measure, to exempt the entire world from judgment (*Nesivos Shalom*).

In the Way of Rabbi Akiva

Nesivos Shalom writes:

> . . . R' Shimon was [also] the one who revealed, and through whom became widely known, the measure of love that exists between the Holy One, Blessed is He, and

1. *Shabbos* 33b.
2. *Succah* 45b.

Israel. *Sefer HaZohar* is replete with references to the great love of Israel towards God and of God towards Israel. For example, "If people would realize the immense love with which God loves Israel, they would roar like a young lion and lift [the hems of] their garments to run after Him."[1]

The source of this outlook regarding God's love toward Israel is the teaching of Rabbi Akiva, teacher of R' Shimon bar Yochai, who declared: "Praiseworthy are you, O Israel! Before Whom do you cleanse yourselves? Who cleanses you? Your Father in Heaven! . . . "[2]

. . . This idea, too, is related to R' Shimon's statement [cited above], "I am able to exempt the entire world from judgment from the day that I was born until now . . . " These spiritual levels are also an outgrowth of the attribute of God's love toward His people which was revealed by R' Shimon. *Love covers over all iniquities.*[3] Through the immense outpouring of love between the Holy One, Blessed is He, and Israel which became manifest through R' Shimon in his day, all judgments were "sweetened" and nullified.

This relates to a concept taught by the Baal Shem Tov, may his merit shield us, on the words, *"HASHEM is your shadow:"*[4] God's conduct toward us is like a shadow which moves according to a person's movements. Therefore, if a Jew perceives, to a degree where it is engraved upon his heart, the intensity of God's love toward him, then in Heaven, too, God acts toward him as a father towards his son . . . and any judgments which may be upon him are "sweetened."

. . . And this is why the people of Israel attach themselves to the light of the holy Sage, Rabbi Shimon bar Yochai, which is particularly radiant on the day of his passing [Lag BaOmer] . . . Every Jew has it within himself to draw close to God, Blessed is His Name, through the

---

1. *Zohar,* Vol. II 5b.
2. *Mishnah Yoma* 8:9. see p. 41.
3. *Proverbs* 10:12.
4. *Psalms* 121:5.

light of Rabbi Shimon bar Yochai . . . Each year on this day, the great light of the hidden portion of Torah flow. [from Heaven], and each person can draw upon himself some of the day's sanctity.

Meron

The celebration on Lag BaOmer at the tomb of R' Shimon bar Yochai is beyond the plane of nature (R' Tzvi Elimelech of Bluzhev in Bnei Yissoschor). [1]

At the time of R' Shimon bar Yochai's passing, a Heavenly voice proclaimed: "Ascend, come and gather for the hilula [joyous celebration] of R' Shimon!"[2] *This Heavenly proclamation was sounded nearly two thousand years ago, yet it reverberates to this day and enters the hearts of the multitudes each year, awakening them to ascend and gather on Lag BaOmer in Meron, the resting place of R' Shimon bar Yochai. There, they rejoice in his joy, on the day of his gladness and festival . . . may his merit shield us and all Israel, Amen (R' Asher Zelig Margulies in Hilula D'Rashbi).*

A Spiritual Landmark

It is a time-honored custom to pray at the graves of *tzaddikim* in the hope that the *tzaddik* will intercede in Heaven on the supplicant's behalf so that his needs will be granted.[3] The tomb of

1. The words ל״ג בָּעוֹמֶר have the same *gematria* as לְמַעְלָה מִן הַטֶּבַע, *beyond the plane of nature* (351 — *R' Moshe Wolfson*).

2. See p. 54.

3. This concept is actually found in the Torah. As one of the Spies who was dispatched by Moses to scout out the Holy Land (*Numbers* Ch.13), Caleb feared that he might be influenced by the wicked designs of the other Spies to disparage the Land. He therefore went to Hebron to the Cave of Machpelah and prostrated himself at the graves of the Patriarchs, saying, "My forefathers! Seek mercy on my behalf, that I be saved from the plans of the Spies" (*Sotah* 34a).

The Talmud relates that on public fast days, the people would go out to the cemeteries. According to one opinion, this was so that "the deceased should beg for mercy on our behalf" (*Taanis* 16a).

Rashi to *Yevamos* 122a, citing *Teshuvos HaGeonim,* writes that "the day on which a great person dies is established as a day of honor for him, and each year on that day, scholars from his surroundings assemble along with the rest of the community and set up a yeshivah by his grave."

R' Shimon bar Yochai and his son, R' Elazar, has been a place of prayer for Jews of all shades and stripes, and a place of study for those who delve into the mystical teachings of the Torah.

Zohar records a number of instances where R' Shimon's disciples visited his tomb. The Talmud relates an incident where R' Yehoshua ben Levi[1] met Elijah the Prophet at "the entrance of the cave of R' Shimon ben Yochai."[2] In *Midrash*[3] it is recorded that on another occasion, Elijah and R' Yehoshua ben Levi were studying the teachings of R' Shimon when R' Yehoshua found difficulty with a particular law. Elijah said to him, "Do you wish to ask this of *Rashbi*?[4] Come, and I will have him appear before you so that you can ask the author of this passage concerning it."

There are many accounts of visits to Meron by outstanding personalities of later generations. The great sixteenth-century kabbalist, R' Yitzchak Luria (the *Arizal*), and his disciples would visit the tomb often. On one such visit, the *Arizal* told his disciples:

> My friends: On this spot, the *Rashbi,* of blessed memory, sat with his disciples, to arrange the *Idra Rabba*[5] — and the remnants of that spiritual light are still present (*Sefer HaKavanos*).

In the diary of his travels, the famed kabbalist R' Moshe Cordovero (*Ramak*)[6] wrote that he prostrated himself at the graves of R' Shimon and his son R' Elazar, and he offered a short prayer there from the depths of his heart.

A wealthy disciple of *Ramak,* R' Avraham Galante,[7] paid for the construction of the building which stands to this day over the cave in which R' Shimon and his son R' Elazar are buried.

---

1. It was R' Yehoshua ben Levi who said, "R' Shimon [bar Yochai] is [sufficiently] worthy to be relied upon in a time of emergency" (*Berachos* 9b — see p. 66).

2. *Sanhedrin* 98a.

3. *Midrash Tehillim* Ch. 36 and *Bereishis Rabbah* 35:2; see also *Sanhedrin* 98a.

4. רַשְׁבִּ״י, *Rashbi* is an acronym for רַבִּי שִׁמְעוֹן בַּר יוֹחַאי.

5. See p. 52.

6. 1522-1570. Among his many writings were *Pardes Rimonim,* a kabbalistic work; and a classic ethical work, *Tomer Devorah.*

7. He authored a number of kabbalistic works, including one on Tractate *Avos.*

R' Moshe Basula writes of his experiences in the year 1522:

> I returned to Meron with ten other people who would go once a month to pray at the tomb of R' Shimon bar Yochai . . . On the fourteenth of Iyar, known as *Pesach Sheini,* more than a thousand people were there, for many came from Damascus along with their wives and children, and most of the communities of Safed and Labukya were there as well. We remained there for two days and two nights, celebrating and rejoicing, and we prayed at the graves of *tzaddikim* there.

Many *tzaddikim* would visit the tomb of R' Shimon two or three times every year. R' Elazar Azkari of Safed,[1] author of *Sefer Charedim,* was a member of the *Arizal's "chaverim,"* a group of pious scholars and disciples. His preface to *Sefer Charedim* begins:

> It happened when the *chaverim* were attentively gathered at the tomb of R' Shimon bar Yochai, delving into his teachings, words of purity, as is our way a few times a year, at regular intervals . . .

R' Yeshayah Horowitz, author of *Shelah,* visited the tomb in the year 1627. He wrote:

> At the grave of R' Shimon bar Yochai they study *Zohar* with awe and fear and great devotion, for many miracles occurred there. One must study the *Zohar* with awe, fear and great devotion and then rejoice in one's heart with a spiritual gladness — and without any mourning or sadness, for *Rashbi* has no desire for this. This is tried and proven. Afterwards, they make vows [or charity] and pray there . . .

The angel known as the *Maggid* who appeared regularly to the author of *Beis Yosef* and *Shulchan Aruch,* R' Yosef Caro,[2] encour-

---

1. See p. 149.

2. 1488-1575. A Heavenly spirit called a *maggid* (lit. one who tells) would make himself known to the *Beis Yosef* only by voice, and would instruct him in kabbalistic interpretation and encourage him in his righteous endeavors. The interpretations on verses in the Torah from the *Maggid* were recorded by the *Beis Yosef* in *Maggid Meisharim.*

aged him to study *Zohar* at the tomb of R' Shimon bar Yochai or in the village near the tomb.

One year during the Succos festival, the *Beis Yosef* and his disciples encircled the tomb of R' Shimon as they held their Four Species. Suddenly it began to rain. The *Beis Yosef* was pained over this, for our Sages teach that rain on Succos is a sign of God's displeasure with our service of Him. "To what is this matter comparable? To a slave who comes to pour wine for his master and he [the master] poured a pitcher on his face."[1]

That year, on the sixth day of Succos, the angel spoke to the *Beis Yosef*:

> The rains which fell were not illustrative of " . . . he poured the pitcher on his face," Heaven forfend. To the contrary, your entreaties were accepted, *Rashbi* and his son rejoiced when you read from *Zohar* at their cave and in the adjacent village. However, when you surrounded the tomb of R' Elazar with the Four Species whose purpose is to grant Heavenly favor for rainfall, the rains were stirred and poured down. Had you encircled [the tomb] one more time, there would have been a torrent of rain like in the days of Choni *HaM'agel*.[2] This is why the rains of blessing came in quick succession, so that you should not encircle any more for them.
>
> Remember this rule: When the world is in need of an abundance of rain, go and encircle the graves of these *tzaddikim,* and your prayers will be answered. And for any trouble that may not[3] befall the community, encircle it seven times and you will be answered. With this you will know that they [R' Shimon and R' Elazar] are very glad when you read the *Zohar* at their tomb or in the nearby village; if you continue to do this, they will reveal to you lofty secrets of the Torah (*Maggid Meisharim*).

1. *Mishnah Succah* 2:9.

2. See *Mishnah Taanis* 3:8.

3. The word "not" is used here as a euphemism, as it is in the *Mishnah* referred to in the previous footnote. The Sages sought to avoid using expressions that signified suffering for Israel.

The Lag BaOmer Pilgrimage

Today, in honor of Lag BaOmer, thousands stream to the tomb of R' Shimon and R' Elazar in Meron. There, the people recite prayers, dance and sing around bonfires and cut the hair of three-year-old boys for the very first time (see below).

It is clear that the Lag BaOmer pilgrimage to Meron is a custom dating back many centuries. The classic commentator on the Mishnah, Rabbi Ovadiah of Bertinoro (Italy) arrived in Jerusalem in 1488. In a letter to his brothers, he wrote: "On the eighteenth of Iyar, the day of [Rabbi Shimon's] passing, they came from everywhere and lit torches . . . for many childless women were redeemed and sick people were cured through the pledges and donations that they offered at this place."

In 1874, the *Rav* of Safed, Rabbi Shmuel Heller, published a pamphlet entitled *Kevod Melachim* (Honor of Kings) which discusses the pilgrimage to Meron. In it he writes:

> I can testify in truth that in my youth I heard from the mouths of venerable rabbis of the *Sefardim,* whose fathers had seen and related to them that the holy rabbi, R' Chaim ben Attar,[1] may his merit shield us, Amen, was once here in the holy city of Safed . . . for the *hilula* (joyous celebration). When he went up to Meron and reached the bottom of the mountain where they ascend [to the tomb], he got down from his donkey and ascended the mountain on his hands and knees; and the whole length of the way he exclaimed . . . "How can I, a lowly creature, enter into the place of fire that gives forth tongues of flames . . . " At the time of the *hilula,* he rejoiced with a very great joy . . .

R' Yeshaya Asher Zelig Margulies writes of the scene at Meron in the first half of this century:

> It is impossible to describe the greatness of this day of joy and the "rejoicing with trembling"[2] which takes place in

1. Author of *Ohr HaChaim,* a classic commentary on the Torah.
2. From *Psalms* 2:11.

Meron on Lag BaOmer. One can actually perceive that it is a day of joy in the upper worlds and in this world . . . a semblance of the World to Come. Some who are there sing and rejoice, exult and delight in dances of holiness, with the joy of singing "*Bar Yochai*" and other holy songs; others stand wrapped in sacred emotions, pouring out their hearts in unceasing streams of tears near the holy burial site of Rabbi Shimon bar Yochai and Rabbi Elazar his son. Wrapped in prayer shawl and *tefillin,* men pray together; still others sit upon the sacred floor and study *Zohar* and other mystical works; others pour out their souls in the recitation of *Psalms.*

Here and there, groups are seen with children, dancing and clapping, holding the little ones on their shoulders and giving them their first haircuts, distributing wine, whiskey and cakes, calling out "*L'Chayim!*" ("To Life!") and exchanging blessings. The crowds refer to these young children as חֲתָנִים דְרַשְׁבִּ״י, *Bridegrooms of Rashbi* (*Hilula D'Rashbi*).

The tens of thousands who stream to Meron to celebrate Lag BaOmer represent the entire spectrum of Jewish custom and observance in the Holy Land. Everyone, it seems, feels drawn to the gravesite of the holy Rabbi Shimon bar Yochai. For as mentioned above, corresponding to the hidden secrets of the Torah which R' Shimon revealed is the hidden spark of holiness in every Jewish soul that can never be extinguished.

The *Arizal* is quoted as having said that on Lag BaOmer R' Shimon bar Yochai stands at his tomb and blesses all who have come to participate in his *hilula.*

Bonfires

Scripture likens Torah to fire; the bonfires which are traditionally lit at Meron and other sites on Lag BaOmer represent the hidden Torah revealed by R' Shimon. Moreover, R' Shimon himself testified, "One day I donned *tefillin* in the cave near Meron; I saw a lamp of fire glowing at the mouth of the cave and I trembled."[1] In *Zohar,*[2] a disciple of R' Shimon records that throughout the day of his teacher's passing, a spiritual fire surrounded his house and that "after the fire left, I saw that the holy luminary, holy of holies, had departed this world . . . "

Chassidic masters attached great spiritual significance to the kindling of these fires. At Meron, it was the custom for decades to auction off the privilege of kindling the bonfire at the tomb of R' Shimon, with the proceeds going to charity. In the nineteenth century, this privilege was purchased permanently by R' Yisrael of Rizhin and to this day, his descendants retain that privilege.[3]

The Hidden Light

The Torah states that on the first day of Creation, God created light and *saw that it was good*.[4] *Rashi* cites the Aggadic interpretation that the primeval light was of an intense spiritual quality and God saw that the wicked were unworthy of enjoying it. Therefore, He hid it away, as it were, for the righteous in the World to Come.

Scripture refers to Torah as a "good teaching."[5] This alludes to the primeval light, the very first item referred to in the Torah as "good," which was hidden in the Torah itself and which can be perceived by those to whom the mystical teachings of Torah are revealed.

This is why R' Shimon bar Yochai is called בּוּצִינָא קַדִּישָׁא, *holy lamp,* and why his classic teachings of Kabbalah are collected under the title of *Sefer HaZohar* (The Book of Radiance), for it is within these teachings that the primeval light is hidden.

---

1. *Zohar,* Vol. III, p. 295.

2. Ibid. p. 291b.

3. R' Avraham Yaakov of Sadigera (a son of R' Yisrael of Rizhin) stated that myriads of Jewish souls attain their *tikun* (spiritual mending) through the kindling in honor of R' Shimon bar Yochai.

Today, the fire at Meron is kindled by the Boyaner *Rebbe,* a descendant of the Rizhiner.

4. *Genesis* 1:4.

5. *Proverbs* 4:2.

Lag BaOmer is seventeen days before the festival of Shavuos. Seventeen is the numerical value of טוֹב, *good.* It is on this day that the spiritual glow of the Festival of Torah begins to manifest itself. Thus, the celebration of Lag BaOmer is truly one of spiritual light, which is represented by the bonfires lit on that day (*Bnei Yissoschor*).[1]

When the Sun Did Not Set

Bnei Yissoschor cites another reason for the custom of lighting bonfires and additional candles on Lag BaOmer. On the day when he departed this world and revealed the esoteric teachings collected in his *Idra Zuta,* R' Shimon bar Yochai said, "Now, it is my desire to reveal secrets . . . This day will not go to its place like any other, for this entire day stands within my domain . . . " Daylight was miraculously extended until R' Shimon had completed transmitting his teachings and had departed this world.

This symbolized that all light in this world is subservient to the light of Torah, particularly the primeval light contained within the mystical teachings of Torah.[2]

---

1. *Bnei Yissoschor* notes that the words [וַיַּרְא אֱלֹהִים] אֶת הָאוֹר [כִּי טוֹב], *[And God saw that]* the light [*was good*] have the numerical value of תַּרְיַ"ג (613) — the number of commandments in the Torah.

2. The Book of *Esther* states: "The Jews had light and gladness, joy and honor" (8:16). R' Yehudah said: *Light* refers to Torah; *gladness* refers to the Festivals; *joy* refers to circumcision; and *honor* refers to *tefillin* (*Megillah* 16b).

Why didn't the *Megillah* simply state, "The Jews had Torah and Festivals, circumcision and *tefillin*"? *Sfas Emes* explains that after the Purim miracle, the Jews attained a heightened realization of the true essence of light, gladness, joy and honor. Originally, they had thought that the true source of light is the sun; after the miracle they realized that Torah is the only true light. Even the most brilliant material light is only a faint approximation in allegorical terms of spiritual light. So it was with the other commandments of which the verse speaks.

Upsherin — The First Haircut

Grooming the Young Trees

☙ When a Jewish boy's hair is cut, it is done according to the Torah law which requires that the *peyos* (lit., corners), the hair of the sideburn area, not be removed.[1] There is a widespread custom to introduce a boy to this *mitzvah* on his third birthday by cutting his hair on that day for the very first time. It is also customary to mark this occasion with celebration.[2]

Many observe this custom on the Lag BaOmer which is closest to the child's third birthday.[3] In Eretz Yisrael, thousands bring their little boys to Meron on Lag BaOmer and cut their hair[4] at the gravesite of Rabbi Shimon bar Yochai. Such was the custom of the *Arizal,* as recorded by his disciple, R' Chaim Vital:

> I have seen my teacher, of blessed memory, going [to the tomb of Rabbi Shimon and his son] these eight years, with his wife and family . . . Furthermore, Rabbi Yonasan Seiges testified to me that one year before I went to study with my teacher, of blessed memory, he took his young son there, along with the rest of his family, and there he cut his

---

1. The Torah states: לֹא תַקִּפוּ פְּאַת רֹאשְׁכֶם, *You shall not round off the edge of your scalp* (*Leviticus* 19:27). Since there is no hair behind the ears, nor on the forehead, cutting the hair off the temples so that it will even the line with the back of the ear and with the forehead is prohibited. The corners of the head extend down to the place where the lower jaw is hinged to the upper jaw. The hair of this part of the head is therefore known as *peyos,* literally, *corners.*

2. As mentioned in *Be'er Heitev* to *Orach Chaim* 531:7 and other sources.

3. Rabbi Chaim Elazar Shapiro, author of *Minchas Elazar,* wrote that if the child is two-and-one-half years old on Lag BaOmer, his first haircut should be given on that day (*Hilula D'Rashbi,* p. 98). It should be noted that there are many variations of this custom; for an extensive treatment of the subject, see *Nitei Gavriel* by Rabbi Gavriel Zinner and *Bein Pesach L'Shavuos* by Rabbi Zvi Cohen.

4. This first haircut is commonly called the "*Upsherin*" ("Haircut"). In Israel, it is known as the חֲלָקָה, *Chalakah.* This term is derived from *Genesis* 27:11, where Jacob refers to himself as an אִישׁ חָלָק, *smooth-skinned man,* in contrast to his brother Esau who was an אִישׁ שָׂעִר, *hairy man.* The removal of the child's long locks of hair is therefore called a חֲלָקָה, *making his head smooth.*

hair in accordance with the well-known custom, and celebrated it as a day of feasting and joy.[1]

An allusion to this custom is found in the Torah where the word וְהִתְגַּלָּח, *and he shall shave* (*Leviticus* 13:33), appears in the Torah scroll with an oversized ג, *gimel*. The numerical value of ג is 3, an allusion that a boy's first haircut should be given at that age (*Ateres Yehoshua*).

Midrashic Source

A number of later commentators[2] cite a Midrashic passage as a source for this custom. The Torah states that all fruits from the first three years of a newly planted tree are forbidden for any use, and those of the fourth year are holy and are to be eaten in Jerusalem.[3] *Midrash* interprets this commandment homiletically as referring to young children:[4]

> [*When you shall come to the land*] *and you shall plant any food tree* — this refers to a young child.
>
> *For three years they shall be closed off to you* — for he cannot converse [intelligently].
>
> *In the fourth year, all its fruits shall be sanctified* — his father shall sanctify him for Torah.
>
> *To laud* HASHEM — for [through his study] the child offers praise unto HASHEM.
>
> (*Yalkut Shimoni, Parashas Kedoshim* §615)

Therefore, at age three, when a boy is to be "sanctified for Torah," his hair is cut according to the way proscribed by the Torah, a *yarmulka* (*kippah*) is placed upon his head for the first time, and he is dressed in his first *tallis katan* (small *tallis*) so that he can fulfill the commandment of *tzitzis*.[5] Then, he is brought

1. *Shaar HaKavanos, Derush Lag BaOmer.*

2. See, for example, Responsa *Arugas HaBosem* (*Orach Chaim* §210); and *Yechaveh Do'as* 5:33.

3. *Leviticus* 19:23-24.

4. Scripture refers to man as *the tree of the field* (*Deuteronomy* 20:1; see *Ibn Ezra*).

5. See "Laws and Customs" in this volume.

into a classroom of young boys where he is given his first "taste" of the Torah's sweetness.

Yalkut Me'am Loez describes the custom of the Jews in eighteenth-century Turkey. Much of what is written there is practiced today in communities around the world:

> When a young boy is brought to a Torah teacher for the first time to learn Torah, his father should arise early and lead him there by the hand. He should offer praise and thanks to the Holy One, Blessed is His Name, for his having merited to bring his son beneath the wings of the Divine Presence. It behooves the boy's father and mother to bathe him and dress him in festive clothing, and the father should hide him beneath his own clothing so that he does not gaze upon any impure sight.
>
> When they arrive at school, the teacher places the child upon his lap. He then takes a board upon which is written the letters of the *Aleph-Beis.* The teacher reads each letter aloud and has the child repeat the letter after him. Then, they recite the verse, תּוֹרָה צִוָּה לָנוּ מֹשֶׁה מוֹרָשָׁה קְהִלַּת יַעֲקֹב (*The Torah that Moshe commanded us is the heritage of the Congregation of Yaakov*).[1] The teacher then places some honey upon the board on which the *Aleph-Beis* letters are displayed, and has the child lick the honey, as a sign that the words of the Torah should be sweet in his mouth. It is customary to bring along honey cookies, milk and fruits, and to distribute them among the children [in the class], while giving some to the little boy as well . . .
>
> It is fitting for a mother and father to fast on this day and pray to God, Blessed is He, that their child should succeed in his Torah studies and grow to be God-fearing. The day on which a child is brought to the classroom for the very first time is as precious before the Holy One, Blessed is

1. *Deuteronomy* 33:4. The *Halachah* states that this verse should be taught to a boy as soon as he begins to talk, as the first fulfillment of the obligation to teach one's son Torah (*Shulchan Aruch, Yoreh De'ah* 245:5). Other laws, such as washing the child's hands according to the prescribed method known as *negel vasser,* are observed by many at an even earlier age. See *Children in Halachah* by Rabbi Simcha Bunim Cohen (Mesorah Publications).

He, as the day when Israel stood at Mount Sinai. This is why the words . . . *and make them known to your children and to your children's children* are juxtaposed with *the day that you stood before HASHEM, your God, at Horeb [Sinai].*[1]

There are places where the custom is to hold a joyous feast on this day; one should not deviate from the custom[2] (*Yalkut Me'am Loez* to *Deuteronomy* 11:19).

While the spiritual milestones in a child's life are opportune occasions for a father and mother to offer prayers on his or her behalf, parents should pray for their children's sake every day of their lives. In *Mishnah Berurah,*[3] the Chofetz Chaim writes:

> Prayer should always be fluent in the mouths of a father and mother to pray for their children that they be students of Torah, *tzaddikim,* men of good character. They should concentrate intently when reciting *Ahavah Rabbah*[4] and in *Bircas HaTorah* when reciting the words, " . . . may we and our offspring [. . . know Your Name and study Your Torah . . .];" and in *Uva L'Tzion* when saying, " . . . so that we do not struggle in vain and produce for futility."

The Chazon Ish once told a man whose child was seriously ill that the prayers of parents on behalf of their children are particularly potent.[5] The Chazon Ish himself composed a prayer to be recited by parents, in which they ask that their sons be diligent and successful in their study of Torah and that they be infused with love and awe of *HASHEM.*[6]

---

1. *Deuteronomy* 4:9-10.

2. As cited above, the *Arizal* celebrated the haircutting of his son as a "day of feasting and joy." In some communities, the feasting is limited to a "*L'Chayim*" of cake and drinks, while among others, a meal is served.

3. 47:10.

4. The blessing which immediately precedes the morning *Shema,* in which we pray, " . . . Our Father, merciful Father, Who acts mercifully, have mercy upon us, instill understanding in our hearts to understand and elucidate, to listen, learn, teach, safeguard, perform, and fulfill all the words of Your Torah's teaching with love."

5. See *Sforno* to *Genesis* 32:1.

6. This prayer appears on p. 193.

In Meron

⌘ As mentioned above, there is a widespread custom in Eretz Yisrael, dating back hundreds of year, to bring boys for their first haircut to Meron on the Lag BaOmer closest to their third birthday. The celebration of the *"chalakah"* of hundreds of young boys at the tomb of R' Shimon bar Yochai is accompanied by euphoric singing and dancing. *Sefer Masa Meron* describes the scene in the year 5648 (1888):

> The precious three-year-old sons of Zion, who are comparable to fine gold![1] I am certain that whoever has not seen this rejoicing has not seen rejoicing in his lifetime.[2] These children are from our Holy Land — Jerusalem, Safed, Tiberias . . . they are dressed in royal garments, their heads wrapped in exquisite coverings . . . those who cannot afford these items borrow them from neighbors, to beautify and decorate their precious sons, the children in whom they delight.
>
> They sit perched atop their fathers' shoulders, their faces shining like the sun in all its strength . . . holding lit torches in their hands. Their fathers, too, are dressed in their Sabbath and holiday finery, dancing and singing a variety of songs in honor of their children's haircuts, offering cake and wine to those assembled, after which they return to their singing —especially *"Bar Yochai,"* in honor of R' Shimon bar Yochai.

In the preface to Responsa *Maharil Paltishan* we find:

> When I was in Meron there were approximately seventy young boys, *Sefardim* and *Ashkenazim,* who were brought from nearby areas. Each son sat atop his father's shoulders as the father danced with joy.

1. Cf. *Lamentations* 4:2.

2. See *Mishnah Succah* 5:1.

The entire family came along for the celebration; each family member would place the boy upon his shoulders and dance with him in middle of the circle. This lasted not only for an hour or two, but in proportion to the level of joy. Every- one together, *Sefardim* and *Ashkenazim,* joined the circle and sang to the accompaniment of music.

The way in which the children sat atop the shoulders of the adults seemed beyond the plane of nature. Anyone who was spiritually uplifted could perceive that this was through the power of the righteous *Rashbi,* [1] who derived pleasure from this celebration, and he took pleasure in the fact that they magnified their rejoicing beyond the norm. As they sat upon the shoulders, the children would grasp the hands of the person carrying them so that they would not fall from the spirited movement of the dancing. Yet, I saw with my own eyes how many children clapped their hands from joy as they sat upon those who danced with them — something which simply was not possible naturally.

The above preface mentions that a boy's first haircut was celebrated joyously not only when it took place on Lag BaOmer, but on any day of the year as well; and that such celebrations were not confined to Meron, but took place anywhere in the Land where an *upsherin* was held. The author expresses wonderment as to why such celebrating is not the norm in the Diaspora as well.

Today, however, many communities in the Diaspora do celebrate the *upsherin* amid great rejoicing.[2]

---

1. An acronym for רבי שמעון בר יוחאי.

2. There are those who bring their three-year-old to Meron on his birthday and cut his hair then. Some who find it difficult to bring the child to Meron cut his hair at the tomb of another tzaddik. Shei'los U'Teshuvos HaRadvaz (vol. II, §608) cites the custom of cutting a three-year-old's hair at the tomb of the prophet Samuel.

In Jerusalem, many celebrate their son's *upsherin* on Lag BaOmer (or on his birthday) at the tomb of Shimon HaTzaddik.

Hints and Allusions

⇝ *Zohar* states that the forty-nine words in verses 13-15 of *Leviticus* Ch. 15 allude to the forty-nine days of *Sefirah*. The thirty-third-word in these verses is מוֹעֵד, *festival*, alluding to the holiday of Lag BaOmer *(R' Gershon Henoch of Radzin)*.

⇝ The Mishnah states: בֶּן שְׁמוֹנֶה עֶשְׂרֵה לְחוּפָּה, *At age eighteen, [one is deemed fit] for the wedding canopy (Avos* 5:21). Homiletically, this alludes to the fact that on the eighteenth of Iyar, Lag BaOmer, mourning is suspended and it is permissible to celebrate weddings (*Sefer Yuchsin* citing *Baal HaMichtam*).

⇝ While all of Torah was taught to Moses at Sinai, until R' Shimon bar Yochai revealed the esoteric teachings to his disciples, only a select few in each generation were privy to them.[1] This is alluded to in the concluding words of the Torah, לְעֵינֵי כָּל יִשְׂרָאֵל, *before the eyes of all Israel,* and its opening word בְּרֵאשִׁית, *in the beginning,* the letters of which can be rearranged to spell אֵת רַשְׁבִּ״י. It was *Rashbi* (R' Shimon bar Yochai) who revealed these hidden teachings *before the eyes of all Israel* (*Siach Yitzchak*).

⇝ The account of R' Shimon bar Yochai's thirteen years in the cave at Lod, when the secrets of the Torah were revealed to him, is recorded on the thirty-third (ל״ג) page of Tractate *Shabbos* and is the thirty-third (לג) passage in the Talmud in which R' Shimon's name is mentioned (*Midos Rashbi* citing R' Avraham Simchah of Barniv).

⇝ The prophet states: [וְ]עֵת צָרָה הִיא לְיַעֲקֹב וּמִמֶּנָּה יִוָּשֵׁעַ, *[And] it shall be a time of trouble for Jacob, but he shall be saved from it* (*Jeremiah* 30:7). The words עֵת צָרָה, *a time of trouble,* have the same *gematria* as רַבִּי שִׁמְעוֹן בֶּן יוֹחַאי (765). In R' Shimon's merit,

1. See p. 51.

the Attribute of Judgment is stilled and though *it is a time of trouble for Jacob* we can be hopeful that *from it he shall be saved (Ahavas Yisrael).*

The *Ben Ish Chai* concludes his *Sefer Hilula Rabba* (on Lag BaOmer) with the following:

> The Torah states:[1] וְנִשְׁמַע קוֹלוֹ בְּבֹאוֹ אֶל הַקֹּדֶשׁ לִפְנֵי ה׳, *Its sound*[2] *shall be heard when he enters the Sanctuary before* HASHEM . . . (In a different context, the words וְנִשְׁמַע קוֹלוֹ could be translated *and his voice shall be heard.*) There is a hint in this verse to *Rashbi* . . . For the word וְנִשְׁמַע has the same letters as שִׁמְעוֹן, *[R'] Shimon,* who merited, on the day of his passing, to reveal heretofore unknown teachings of supreme secrets. *And his voice was heard* before those Above and those below on the day of his *hilula* (joyous celebration), *when he entered the Sanctuary* [of Heaven] *before* HASHEM. May it be God's will that the merit of R' Shimon's teachings and good deeds shield us and all Israel, Amen.

1. *Exodus* 28:35.

2. The sound of the bells on the *me'il* (robe) of the *Kohen Gadol.*

Selected Laws and Customs

Selected Laws and Customs

The laws of mourning during the *Sefirah* period and their suspension on Lag BaOmer are found in *Shulchan Aruch, Orach Chaim* Ch. 493 and its commentaries. In preparing the digest below, extensive use has been made of *Sefiras HaOmer* (English) by Rabbi Shimon Eider and two comprehensive Hebrew works: *Bein Pesach L'Shavuos* by Rabbi Zvi Cohen (Bnei Brak 1985) and *Nitei Gavriel* by Rabbi Gavriel Zinner (New York 1996).

Few areas of Jewish observance are as subject to custom as the weeks of *Sefirah* and Lag BaOmer. All questions regarding practical observance should be directed to a competent halachic authority.

The Nightly Count

Throughout *Sefirah*, one should be careful from the start of twilight and on not to say in conversation, "Tonight is the .... day [of the *Omer*]," for in so doing he has effectively counted that night's count and will not be able to recite the blessing on the *mitzvah* when he counts at the conclusion of *Maariv*.[1] Therefore, it is important that from the start of twilight on the eve of Lag BaOmer, one should not say, "Tonight is Lag BaOmer."[2]

Increasing of Joy

On Lag BaOmer there is an increasing of joy, for on that day the disciples of Rabbi Akiva ceased to die.[3] We have discussed at length additional reasons for joy on this day.[4]

Tachanun is not recited on this day, nor is it recited at *Minchah* of the previous day, as on any day which precedes a festival.[5] When Lag

1. Shulchan Aruch, Orach Chaim 489:4.

2. *Bein Pesach L'Shavuos* 17:13. Some hold that one should be careful in this regard from *plag haminchah* and on (1¼ seasonal hours prior to day's end).

3. *Rama, Orach Chaim* 493:2.

4. See p. 36 and pp. 43-61.

5. *Levush* 493:4; *Pri Megadim, Mishbetzos Zahav* 492:1; *Mishnah Berurah* 493:9 and other sources.

BaOmer falls on Sunday, the "*Tzidkasecha*" verses normally recited at *Minchah* of Shabbos are not said.[1]

Many recite *Psalm* 20 [. . . לַמְנַצֵּחַ] at *Shacharis* as usual.[2] However, in Sefardic and chassidic communities, the custom is not to recite this psalm, as on festivals.[3]

Even those who fast on a *yahrtzeit* do not do so if the *yahrtzeit* is on Lag BaOmer.[4] There are varying customs with regard to a bride and groom fasting on the day of their wedding.[5]

Weddings and Haircuts

There are varying customs as to when during *Sefirah* the mourning period for the disciples of Rabbi Akiva is observed. According to the author of *Shulchan Aruch*, R' Yosef Caro, the disciples ceased dying on the thirty-fourth day of the *Sefirah* period.[6] Regarding mourning, we apply the principle of מִקְצָת הַיּוֹם כְּכוּלּוֹ, *part of the day is counted as the whole day*. Thus, according to this opinion, it is from the day after Lag BaOmer and on that wedding and haircuts are permitted. *Sefardim* follow this opinion, though they, too, celebrate Lag BaOmer as the *hilula* (joyous celebration) of R' Shimon bar Yochai.

Rama follows the opinion that the disciples ceased dying on the thirty-third day of the *Omer* period.[7] Following the rule of מִקְצָת הַיּוֹם

1. *Levush* ibid. *Shulchan Aruch* (*Orach Chaim* 292:2) states that these verses are not recited when *Tachanun* would not be said had it been a weekday.

2. *Pri Megadim, Eishel Avraham* 493:3. See *Rama* 131:1.

3. This opinion is found in *Pri Chadash* 131:1 and other sources.

4. *Leket Yosher, Orach Chaim* p. 97.

5. See *Bein Pesach L'Shavuos* p. 309.

6. *Orach Chaim* 493:1-2.

7. *Rama* (493:3 as elucidated by *Be'ur Halachah* s.v. יש נוהגין) cites another opinion: R' Akiva's disciples died on the days of *Sefirah* which were neither Sabbaths nor holidays (including Rosh Chodesh). This would exclude sixteen days: the seven days of Pesach (beginning from the second day of Pesach); six remaining Sabbaths; two days of Rosh Chodesh Iyar and one day of Rosh Chodesh Sivan. What remains is thirty-three days on which they died. According to this opinion, the deaths stretched across the entire period from the end of Pesach until Shavuos [excluding holidays]. It was accepted, according to this view, to observe a thirty-three day mourning period commencing with the second of Iyar and ending on *erev* Shavuos. To one of these days, Lag BaOmer, we apply the rule of מִקְצָת הַיּוֹם כְּכוּלּוֹ and permit celebrations and haircutting.

There is a variation of the above custom which prohibits weddings and haircuts on

כְּכוּלּוֹ, he rules that haircuts are permitted from daytime of Lag BaOmer and on. *Mishnah Berurah*[1] cites the opinion of some later commentators that haircuts are permitted on the night of Lag BaOmer as well. With regard to weddings, however, he cites *Eliyahu Rabba*: "I have not seen a lenient opinion [regarding weddings] except on the day of Lag BaOmer, not on the night when it begins. However, when Lag BaOmer falls on Friday and it is very difficult to make a wedding on that day, it is possible that one may be lenient and celebrate a wedding on the previous night."

R' Moshe Feinstein,[2] however, cites the opinion of *Chasam Sofer* that there is greater room for leniency regarding weddings than regarding haircuts. Accordingly, he rules that weddings may be held on the night on which Lag BaOmer is ushered in. This is the opinion of some earlier authorities as well.[3]

When a wedding is held on the night on which Lag BaOmer begins, the *chuppah* (wedding ceremony) and playing of music cannot begin until nightfall, which halachically begins with the emergence of three medium-size stars.[4] When a wedding is held on the day of Lag BaOmer, the *chuppah* must be before sunset, while the meal, music

---

the two days of Rosh Chodesh Iyar and permits them during שְׁלֹשֶׁת יְמֵי הַגְבָּלָה, the three days which precede Shavuos.

For kabbalistic reasons, the *Arizal* prohibited haircutting throughout the *Sefirah* period until *erev Shavous* (*Shaarei Teshuvah* 493:8). Some hold that this prohibition applies to weddings as well. However, others are of the opinion that the joy of Lag BaOmer allows for weddings even according to the *Arizal*. This opinion is related in the name of R' Chaim of Sanz (author of *Divrei Chaim*), who is reported to have celebrated the wedding of one of his children on Lag BaOmer. See *Nitei Gavriel* p. 214 and *Bein Pesach L'Shavuos* p. 311.

One should also note that many follow the ruling of *R' Yehudah HaChassid* (in *Sefer Chassidim*) not to cut hair or nails on Rosh Chodesh, even when it falls on *erev* Shabbos.

1. 493:11.

2. *Igros Moshe, Orach Chaim I*, §159.

3. *Pri Chadash* 493:2; *Shulchan Aruch HaRav* 493:5; *Mor U'Ketziah, Machzik Berachah* 493:5; and other sources.

4. *Pri Chadash*, who permits weddings on the night of Lag BaOmer, offers the reason of מִקְצָת הַלַּיְלָה כְּכוּלּוֹ, *a portion of the night is like the entire night*, with regard to mourning. (Though this is not the accepted opinion regarding mourning for a deceased, *Pri Chadash* states that with regard to the mourning of *Sefirah*, it may be relied upon.) It follows then, that the night must begin before the start of the ceremony (see *Sefer Nitei Gavriel*).

and dancing may take place after dark, though it is no longer Lag BaOmer.[1]

Even according to Sefardic custom not to cut hair until the thirty-fourth day of *Sefirah*, if Lag BaOmer falls on Friday, haircuts are permitted in honor of the Sabbath.[2]

When Lag BaOmer falls on Sunday, Ashkenazic custom permits cutting hair on Friday in honor of the Sabbath.[3]

The Hilula (Joyous Celebration) of R' Shimon

Celebrations are held at Meron, throughout Eretz Yisrael and in many communities throughout the Diaspora, marking the day on which R' Shimon bar Yochai departed this world and revealed mystical teachings of the Torah.[4] Celebrations, highlighted by singing and dancing, are usually held on the night of Lag BaOmer following the counting of the *Omer*.

Sefer Hilula D'Rashbi states: "It is a custom in Israel to ascend on this day to [R' Shimon's] holy gravesite in Meron. One should conduct himself with fear and dread, sanctity and purity, as is befitting this holy place. One should distance himself from lightheadedness and the like — *in the very place where you rejoice, there you should tremble.*"[5]

One can also participate in the *hilula* of R' Shimon by studying his many teachings which are recorded in Talmudic and Midrashic sources.[6]

---

1. *Igros Moshe, Even HaEzer I*, §97. It would seem that according to the custom cited above that the mourning period begins with the first day of *Sefirah* and ends on Lag BaOmer, weddings should be permitted from Lag BaOmer and on. However, *Taz* (493:2) states that while haircutting is permitted, Ashkenazic custom is not to hold weddings from after Lag BaOmer and on (presumably until Rosh Chodesh Sivan — see *Igros Moshe, Orach Chaim* I, §159). This, *Taz* explains, is because the worst massacres of the Crusades happened in the weeks between Pesach and Shavuos, and therefore some mourning is still in place after Lag BaOmer regardless of one's custom in observing the mourning for Rabbi Akiva's disciples.

2. *Shulchan Aruch* 493:2.

3. *Rama* 493:2.

4. See *Shaar HaKavanos* (by the *Arizal's* disciple R' Chaim Vital), p. 87a.

5. *Berachos* 30b. Thousands visit the tomb of R' Shimon throughout the year. *Arizal* is quoted as having advised that one should not visit the tomb alone.

6. R' Asher Zelig Margulies in *Hilula D'Rashbi*. See "Teachings of R' Shimon Bar Yochai" in this volume.

Some have the custom of studying the esoteric teachings of R' Shimon bar Yochai found in *Zohar* and *Tikkunei Zohar*[1] — especially the *Idra Zuta* which he revealed on the day of his passing.[2]

In the Diaspora, many visit the graves of *tzaddikim* on Lag BaOmer.[3] By complementing such pilgrimages with the giving of charity for the poor of Israel, one is considered as having participated in the *hilula* of R' Shimon.[4]

A Day of Light

In Meron and in communities throughout Israel and beyond, bonfires are lit on the night of Lag BaOmer; in many synagogues, additional candles are lit on this day. These flames represent the hidden light of the teachings of Kabbalah; the fire which surrounded R' Shimon bar Yochai's place of learning on that fateful day when he departed this world;[5] and the tradition that on that day, daylight was miraculously extended to allow R' Shimon to complete the transmission of his esoteric teachings to his disciples.[6]

When kindling a flame on Lag BaOmer, it is proper to say: הֲרֵינִי מַדְלִיק נֵר לִכְבוֹד הַתַּנָּא רַבִּי שִׁמְעוֹן בַּר יוֹחָאי, *I am lighting a candle in honor of the Tanna Rabbi Shimon Bar Yochai.*[7]

It is also customary to sing *"Bar Yochai"* and other songs in honor

---

1. See p. 175.

2. *Chida* in *Moreh Etzba* (8:223) and *Kaf HaChaim* 493:27.

It is particularly appropriate to study R' Shimon's teachings at his tomb. *Pesikta Rabasi* (Ch. 12) states: "If one is walking among graves and knows that a *tzaddik* is buried there, he should make mention of his deeds." *Radal* adds: "This appears to be a source for the custom in Eretz Yisrael, may it be rebuilt speedily and in our time, to read at the graves of *tzaddikim* sentences and passages that relate to the *tzaddik* buried there."

It is related that every year on Lag BaOmer, the Chassidic master R' Baruch of Mezhibuzh (a grandson of the Baal Shem Tov) would celebrate his completing the study of *Sefer HaZohar*. After the *siyum* (completion), he would take a volume of *Sefer HaZohar* in his hands and dance with it for hours.

3. *Nitei Gavriel* citing numerous Chassidic sources.

4. Ibid. citing *Berachah Sheleimah*.

5. See p. 54.

6. *Bnei Yissoschor* and other sources. See p. 84.

7. *Mishmeres Shalom*.

of R' Shimon bar Yochai.[1] Masters of Kabbalah taught that the words of this song have the power to illuminate one's soul. Many sing these songs at a bonfire.

In Chassidic courts and elsewhere, festive meals are held at which Lag BaOmer songs are sung[2] and words of Torah are heard. *Sefer Chesed V'Emes* states: "One who holds a festive *seudas mitzvah* (*mitzvah* banquet) in honor of the joy of R' Shimon bar Yochai on the day of his *hilula* is praiseworthy — but the *seudah* should be conducted in a spirit of Torah, with awe of God upon one's countenance, and with joy which stems from performing a *mitzvah*."

Week-Long Celebration

R' Chaim Vital testified that his master and teacher the *Arizal* visited the tomb of R' Shimon bar Yochai in honor of Lag BaOmer and remained there for three consecutive days. The Chassidic masters taught that the spiritual aura which is manifest at Meron on Lag BaOmer, the *yahrtzeit* of R' Shimon, is present for an entire week: from three days preceding Lag BaOmer until the third day following it.[3] This is likened to the aura of the Sabbath, which is manifest to some degree beginning on Wednesday prior to the Sabbath and remains to some degree until the conclusion of the Tuesday which follows it.[4]

Rabbi Akiva and His Disciples

Some have the custom on Lag BaOmer to visit the graves of Rabbi Akiva[5] and his disciple, R' Meir,[6] in Tiberias; and that of R' Akiva's disciple R' Yehudah bar Ilai in Meron. The writings of Kab-

1. See p. 158.

2. See *Rama*, 670:2.

3. *Sh'eilos U'Teshuvos Nachalah Yisrael* and other sources.

4. This has halachic ramifications; see *Mishnah Berurah* 248:8 and 299:16.

5. The teacher of Rabbi Shimon bar Yochai. See p. 43.

6. Known as *R' Meir Baal HaNeis* (R' Meir the Controller of Miracles), his maxim, אֱלָהָא דְמֵאִיר עֲנֵנִי, *God of Meir answer me* (see *Avodah Zara* 18a), remains the hope of Jews in distress to this day.

balah state that Rabbi Akiva and the five disciples through whom his teachings were transmitted to the next generation rejoice in Heaven on this day.[1]

In communities throughout the world, it is customary to sing "*Amar Rabbi Akiva,*" a teaching of Rabbi Akiva found in the last *mishnah* of *Masechta Yoma,* on Lag BaOmer.[2]

Yahrtzeit of the Rama

Lag BaOmer is also the *yahrtzeit* of R' Moshe Isserles, the famed *Rama.*[3] Over the centuries, this day had been one on which scores have visited *Rama's* grave in Cracow where he had served as *Rav* and where his famed writings were compiled.

R' Moshe Isserles was born in the year 5290 (1530) into one of the most prominent families of the Cracow Jewish community; his surname, Isserles, is actually an allusion to his father's first name, Yisrael *Isser.*[4] As a young man, he was appointed Rav of Cracow, an astoundingly prestigious position for someone his age. He also established a Talmudic academy in Cracow, where he delivered brilliant discourses and also supplied the students' material needs.

Among *Rama's* most famous disciples were: R' Mordechai Yafeh, author of *Levush;* R' Yehoshua Falik *HaKohen,* author of *Sefer Me'iras Einayim (Sma);* R' Hirsh Shor, one of the teachers of R' Yoel Sirkis, the author of *Bach;* and R' Avraham Horowitz, whose son R' Yeshayah authored *Shnei Luchos HaBris (Shelah).*

A prolific writer, *Rama* is the teacher of all future generations by way of his commentary to *Tur* and *Beis Yosef,* entitled *Darchei Moshe;* and especially, by the work which is based upon *Darchei Moshe* — his glosses to the code of Jewish law, *Shulchan Aruch,* which he entitled *Sefer HaMapah.*[5]

Since R' Yosef Caro, in formulating his halachic code, adopted the

---

1. *Sefer Hilula Rabba.*

2. See p. 157.

3. רמ״א, *Rama,* is an acronym for רַבִּי מֹשֶׁה אִיסֶרְלִיש.

4. See *Stories* section for a fascinating account concerning the *Rama's* father.

5. See *The Early Acharonim* by Rabbi Hersh Goldwurm (Mesorah Publications) for a discussion of *Rama's* other writings.

practices of Sephardic communities, it was not usable by Ashkenazic Jewry until *Rama* added his work, in the form of notes inserted into *Shulchan Aruch's* text. Where there is conflict between R' Yosef Caro and *Rama*, *Ashkenazim* generally follow *Rama's* decision. But the accomplishments *Rama* achieved with his notes transcended the needs of Ashkenazic Jewry. His notes elevated *Shulchan Aruch* from an individual expression of halachic law to an authoritative work of *halachah* worthy of use by all of Jewry. It is probably this unique aspect of this joint work which contributed greatly to its eventual universal acceptance as the ultimate halachic authority.

In the words of R' Hersh Goldwurm:

> On a spiritual level, *Rama's* role may perhaps be compared to that of Beis Hillel in the Mishnah, whose rulings, the Talmud states, were accepted because of their humility. It was surely *Rama's* humility which induced him to express his opinion in the form of glosses to a contemporary work rather than opt for personal accomplishment in the form of an original, individual work. The very name he gave his glosses demonstrates this spirit. They are aptly named *Sefer HaMapah* (The Covering); they are merely the "cloth" which covers the "set table" ("*Shulchan Aruch*") and lends it grace.
>
> ... The reverence for *Rama* is attested to by the yearly pilgrimages to his grave on his *yahrtzeit*, which is observed to this day. Jewry's appreciation for his accomplishments is fittingly summed up in the inscription which appears on his tombstone: "From Moshe *[Rambam]* to Moshe *[Rama]*, there was no one like Moshe."[1]

Prayers at Gravesites

One who visits the graves of *tzaddikim* to offer prayers should *not* pray to the deceased. Rather, he should pray to God that He should grant compassion in the *tzaddik's* merit. It is proper to come before the grave and say, "I ask of the soul of the *tzaddik* buried here, that it

1. This is the inscription that appears on the tombstone of *Rambam*, where "From Moshe" refers to Moshe *Rabbeinu* (Moses).

should pray on my behalf before the Holy One, Blessed is He . . . "[1]

It is proper to donate charity to the poor before praying at a gravesite.[2]

Upsherin/First Haircut

The custom of cutting a boy's hair for the first time on Lag BaOmer is discussed at length in the *Insights* section of this volume (see pp. 85-90). Below are some laws and customs related to the *upsherin*:

It is proper to wash the child's hands after the haircut, as is required for an adult, or a child who has reached the age of *chinuch*, training.[3]

From the time that the child's hair is cut, he should be trained to wear a *yarmulka* (*kippah*).[4] The general custom is to also introduce the child at this time to the *mitzvah* of wearing *tzitzis*.[5]

The cutting of the child's hair is done amidst great joy. Some actually cut the first hairs in a synagogue in the presence of those assembled.[6] Many honor a renowned Torah scholar with cutting the first hairs, followed by grandparents, then other relatives and friends.[7]

In many Chassidic circles, the first cut of hair is taken from the center of the child's head just above the hairline, where he will one day wear *tefillin*.[8] Others take the first hair from the area near the *peyos*, since that is the *mitzvah* to which the child is now being introduced.[9]

---

1. *Sefer Chagim U'Zemanim* citing *Ben Ish Chai.*

2. *Mateh Moshe* quoting *Maharshal.* Note the words of *Rama* regarding the laws of *erev* Rosh Hashanah: "There are places where the custom is to visit graves and offer abundant prayers there, and to give charity to the poor" (*Orach Chaim* 581:4).

3. *Nitei Gavriel,* based on *Shulchan Aruch, Orach Chaim* 4:18.

4. *Sefer Chinuch Yisrael,* p. 239. *Shulchan Aruch* states: "One should not walk four *amos* with his head uncovered, to show honor for the Divine Presence" (*Orach Chaim* 2:6). *Mishnah Berurah* (§11) adds: "It is the way of piousness [to wear a *yarmulka*) even when walking less than four *amos,* and even while sleeping at night . . . *Magen Avraham* writes that even [young] children should be trained to cover their heads so that the fear of Heaven should be upon them, as the Sages state (*Shabbos* 156a), 'Cover your head so that the fear of Heaven should be upon you.' "

The word *yarmulka* is a contraction of יְרֵא מַלְכָּא, *one who fears the King.*

5. *Shaarei Teshuvah* 17:2; *Aruch HaShulchan* 17:5.

6. *Sdei Chemed, Beis HaKnesses* §10.

7. *Shaarei Yerushalayim.*

8. *Yalkut HaTaspores.*

9. Such was the custom of R' Menachem Mendel Schneerson of Lubavitch.

Others take the first hair from the top of the head where the hair is usually thickest.[1]

In a number of prominent prewar communities in Europe, it was customary for parents to donate charity on the day of the *upsherin* as a source of merit for the child. This was also done on the day when the child began to read from a *siddur* and when he began to learn *Mishnayos* or *Gemara*.[2]

In many communities, a child on the day of his *upsherin* is brought to a *tzaddik* to receive his blessings.

Bows and Arrows

It has been the way of many Chassidic masters to go outdoors on Lag BaOmer and make use of a bow and arrow. To this day, this custom is popular in Chassidic grade schools and other yeshivos where children are often taken on field trips on Lag BaOmer.

One reason for this practice is the tradition that as long as Rabbi Shimon bar Yochai lived, a rainbow did not appear in the sky (*Yerushalmi Berachos* 9:1). The rainbow is the sign of God's covenant with Noah that never again would all of mankind be destroyed (*Genesis* 9:11-12). During Rabbi Shimon's lifetime this sign was not necessary, for his merit was sufficient to shield the world from destruction.

Zohar (*Parashas Vayikra*) states: "A sign of a pure *chasid* (exceptionally righteous person) is that no rainbow appeared in his lifetime, for the world did not need this sign as long as he was alive. And who is such a *tzaddik*? One who seeks mercy for the world and has the power to shield the entire world — such as R' Shimon bar Yochai, in whose lifetime the world did not need this sign."

The use of bows and arrows on Lag BaOmer symbolize that Rabbi

---

1. The custom of the *Admorim* of Skulen. See *Kedushas Levi* to *Exodus* 20:2.

2. *Mekoros HaChinuch L'Yisrael*. The day of his *upsherin*, on which he was brought to a Torah teacher, was considered the day on which he was introduced to the study of *Chumash*. Today, the official learning of *Chumash* which follows the reading from a *siddur* is celebrated in school (see also page 87 in this volume).

Some have a custom to weigh the hair which has been cut off and to contribute its weight in gold or silver to *tzedakah* as a *segulah* (auspicious omen) that the child merit to be Godfearing and enjoy longevity (*Segulos Yisrael* 3:25; see also *Sh'eilos U'Teshuvos Ridvaz*, Vol. II §428).

Shimon's spiritual stature took the place of the bow (*Bnei Yissoschor*).

In *Zohar*, R' Shimon bar Yochai is quoted as telling his son R' Elazar that a brilliant rainbow is a sign of the Messiah's imminent arrival. The rainbow's brilliance at that time will indicate that the hidden primeval light which God concealed within the mystical teachings of Torah will then be revealed to all. On Lag BaOmer, writes *Bnei Yissoschor*, we recall this by using bows and arrows.

The letters of the word קֶשֶׁת, *bow*, when rearranged, form the initials of קְוֻצּוֹתָיו תַּלְתַּלִּים שְׁחוֹרוֹת (lit., *His locks are wavy and black*[1]). The Sages interpret these words as an allegory for the crowns of the Torah scroll which have hidden within them mounds and mounds of Torah laws.[2] This alludes to the greatness of R' Shimon bar Yochai (and his teacher Rabbi Akiva) who were able to derive mounds of laws from every point of every letter in the Torah (*Gal Peninim*).

Dairy

In some Chassidic circles, there is a custom to eat dairy on Lag BaOmer. In the writings of Kabbalah, wine and blood symbolize judgment, while water and milk represent compassion. This is one reason why it is customary to eat dairy on Shavuos. As noted above, the spiritual aura of Shavuos begins to manifest itself on Lag BaOmer, a day on which an abundance of Divine compassion flows from Above.[3]

---

1. *Song of Songs* 5:11.

2. The words קְוֻצּוֹתָיו תַּלְתַּלִּים are understood to mean that it is possible to derive עַל כָּל קוֹץ וְקוֹץ, *from every single point* [of every letter in the Torah], תִּילֵי תִּילִים שֶׁל הֲלָכוֹת, *mounds and mounds of laws* (*Eruvin* 21b).

3. See *Sefer Nitei Gavriel*, p. 290.

Teachings of Rabbi Shimon bar Yochai

Talmudic and Midrashic Selections

Aggadic Accounts

Talmudic and Midrashic Selections

R' Yochanan said in the name of R' Shimon bar Yochai: Any Torah scholar whose teachings are repeated on this world, his lips murmur in the grave [i.e. in the next world — Rabbeinu Gershom] (Yevamos 97a). [1]

◆ It is related that R' Avraham Mordechai Alter of Gur, author of *Imrei Emes,* was once journeying to Tiberias to visit the tomb of Rabbi Akiva when he was overcome by weakness. He told his attendant, "Come, let us return home; there, we will be able to reach R' Akiva through an easier method," meaning, through the study of his teachings.

It is in this vein that the kabbalist R' Asher Zelig Margulies writes: One who is unable to visit Meron on Lag BaOmer should study the teachings of R' Shimon bar Yochai which are scattered throughout the Talmud and *Midrash.* [2]

In *Midos Rashbi,* R' Margulies collects and comments on these teachings — a total of more than two thousand! Below, we offer a small selection of the teachings of R' Shimon, followed by Aggadic accounts from his life, found in *Midrash* and *Zohar,* which contain vital lessons.

Three Precious Gifts

R' Shimon bar Yochai said: The Holy One, Blessed is He, gave three good gifts to Israel, and He gave all of them through suffering. They are: Torah, the Land of Israel and

1. The Talmud deduces this teaching from the verse "And [the words of] your palate shall be . . . stirring the lips of those who sleep" (*Song of Songs* 7:10).

2. *Hilula D'Rashbi. Kol Aryeh* finds an allusion to this in the Talmudic statement: "R' Shimon is worthy of being relied upon in his presence and not in his presence" (*Pesachim* 51b). While the statement is intended in a halachic sense, it can be interpreted homiletically: R' Shimon's merit can achieve salvation both at his tomb in Meron (*in his presence*) and anywhere in the world for those who attach themselves to the light of his teachings.

the World to Come.

Torah — as it says, "Fortunate is the man whom God afflicts, and whom You teach from Your Torah.[1]

The Land of Israel — as it says, "Just as a father chastises his son, so Hashem, your God, chastises you,"[2] *and it is written immediately after that verse, "For Hashem, your God, is bringing you to a good land."*

The World to Come — as it says, "For the commandments are a candle, and the Torah is light, and reproofs of instruction are the way of life"[3] (*Berachos* 5a).

☙ How appropriate that the very first teaching of R' Shimon bar Yochai found in the Talmud states that Torah is acquired through suffering. It was R' Shimon who told his son-in-law R' Pinchas ben Yair, "Fortunate are you for having seen me like this,[4] for had you not seen me in such a state, you would not have found within me the level of Torah knowledge which I now possess." The suffering which he had endured during his thirteen years in the cave had brought him to awesome heights of Torah wisdom.

The Talmud[5] relates that when R' Yose the grandson of R' Shimon died, it was decided to bring him to the tomb of his father (R' Elazar) and grandfather for burial. When the procession arrived at the tomb in Meron, they found a serpent encircling the cave. They said to it, "Serpent, serpent, open your mouth and let a son enter to his father!" However, the serpent did not open for them and they had to bury R' Yose elsewhere. The people took this as an indication that R' Yose had not attained the level of his father, and hence was not permitted to be buried with him.

---

1. *Psalms* 52:12. Indulgence in physical pleasures leads to the neglect of Torah study, as implied by the Mishnah (*Avos* 6:4), "This is the way of Torah: Eat bread with salt, drink water in small measure. . ." (*Maharsha*).

2. *Deuteronomy* 8:5. The Land of Israel was not given merely for the sake of partaking of its good fruits and indulging in its delights, for that can lead to rebellion against God [see *Deuteronomy* 8:12-14] (*Maharsha*).

3. *Proverbs* 6:23. חַיִּים, *life,* is a reference to the World to Come, which is the eternal life. Accordingly, the verse teaches that דֶּרֶךְ חַיִּים, *the way of life* (i.e. the way to the life of the World to Come), is earned through *reproofs of instruction* (i.e. afflictions), which cleanse a person of his sin (*Rashi, Maharsha*).

4. With his skin cracked from his years spent in the sand; see p. 49.

5. *Bava Metzia* 85a.

However, a Heavenly voice proclaimed, "It is not because this one is greater than that one; rather, this one [R' Elazar] endured the discomfort of the cave, whereas this one [R' Yose] did not endure the discomfort of the cave."

Communal Prayer

R' Yochanan said in the name of R' Shimon bar Yochai: What is the meaning of that which is written, "But as for me, my prayer to you, Hashem, at a favorable time"?[1] *When is it a* favorable time? *At the time the congregation prays* (*Berachos* 7b-8a).

☙ This teaches that one who prays alone should make sure that his prayers coincide with those of the congregation.[2] The Talmud goes on to stress the advantages of congregational prayer.

Zohar comments on the verse, "He turned to the prayer of the devastated one and has not despised their prayer":[3] The verse begins in the singular (*devastated one*) and ends in the plural (*their prayer*). *Zohar* explains that when a man prays alone, God rivets His scrutiny on the supplicant and his failings come to light. Indeed, God does not ignore or reject the prayer of the wretched individual; He does *turn to it,* but after consideration and analysis of merit God may very well decide not to accept it.

However, when a *minyan* (quorum) of Jews gather to pray, God always views them favorably. He never rejects their prayer.[4]

---

1. *Psalms* 69:14. In a monograph entitled *Maamar Eis Ratzon,* R' Asher Zelig Margulies lists communal prayer among seventeen "favorable times." His list draws upon Talmudic sources as well as works of Kabbalah and Chassidus. *Maamar Eis Ratzon* is printed at the back of *Midos Rashbi* (1998 edition published in Monroe, N.Y.) and the Eshkol edition of *Shaarei Kedushah* by R' Chaim Vital.

2. See *Hagahos HaGra* for an alternate reading of the text.

3. *Psalms* 102:18.

4. *Chazah Tzion* explains that whenever God observes a group of Jews, He identifies them with their glorious ancestry and in the merit of their forefathers they always curry Divine favor. The initial letters of the phrase וְלֹא בָזָה אֶת תְּפִילָּתָם, *and has not despised their prayers,* form the word אָבוֹת, *Patriarchs.*

The Unity of the Jewish People

Chizkiyah taught: "Israel is [like] a scattered sheep."[1] *When one of a sheep's organs become afflicted, all its organs are affected.*[2] *Similarly, all of Israel may suffer retribution because of one Jew's sins.*

R' Shimon ben Yochai taught: This can be likened to a group traveling aboard a ship. One of the travelers begins to drill a hole in the floor beneath him. His companions cry out, "What are you doing?" "What do you care?" he responds, "I'm only drilling beneath my seat!" "But the ship will become flooded and all of us will drown!" the others retort (*Vayikra Rabbah* 4:6).

☙ The Chofetz Chaim relates this teachings to the verse, "All the souls of the house of Jacob who came to Egypt, seventy."[3] The Hebrew word for *souls* is נְפָשׁוֹת. Yet, in this verse, the singular form, נֶפֶשׁ, is used, alluding to the fact that in Heaven, the souls of the people of Israel are like a single body comprised of many individual parts, each distinct and unique. It is only in this world, where each soul is clothed in its own physical garb and is involved in its own personal life, that one can see himself as a separate entity, apart from his fellow Jew. In truth, however, all Jews are one in a very real sense. Therefore, our deeds and misdeeds affect one another in a very profound way.

The Sabbath and Israel

Rabbi Shimon bar Yochai said: All the mitzvos which God gave Israel were given in the open, with the exception of the Sabbath which was given in private, as it is written, "Between Me and Israel it is an eternal sign"[4] (*Beitzah* 16a).

---

1. *Jeremiah* 50:17.
2. I.e., they become inflamed (*Maharzu*).
3. *Genesis* 46:27.
4. *Exodus* 31:17.

As *Rabbeinu Bachya* points out, R' Shimon cannot mean that the commandment to keep the Sabbath was given in private, for the *mitzvah* of Shabbos was included among the Ten Commandments which were given amid thunder and lightning and the transmission of which was known throughout the world. The Talmud itself alludes to this point, and in one interpretation, explains R' Shimon's statement as a reference to the נְשָׁמָה יְתֵירָה, *additional soul,* which each Jew is granted at the Sabbath's onset.

As the Sabbath begins, a Jew experiences a tremendous spiritual awakening. His earthly being is diminished and his heavenly soul yearns to be closer to its Creator, to delight with the source whence it came. This awakening is unique to the day of Sabbath and it is this uplifting of the soul which is the essence of the *additional soul.*

This concept is related to another teaching of R' Shimon:

> *R' Shimon bar Yochai said: The Sabbath came before the Holy One, Blessed is He, and said: "Master of the Universe, for each day of the week there is a mate [Sunday and Monday, Tuesday and Wednesday, etc.], but I have no mate."*
>
> *The Holy One, Blessed is He, replied, "The Nation of Israel will be your mate"* (*Bereishis Rabbah* 11:8).

The Sabbath represents the pinnacle of *dveikus,* spiritual attachment; to the degree that one attaches himself to the Sabbath, he attaches himself to the One Above.

The 613 commandments are, essentially, varying means through which one attains attachment to God. In this sense, the Sabbath is the soul of all the *mitzvos* and is equal to all of them combined (*Nesivos Shalom*).[1]

The Sanctity of the Sabbath

> *R' Shimon said: "A psalm, a song for the day of Sabbath."*[2] *This psalm was said by Adam, for the day of Sabbath came*

1. See *Rashi* to *Numbers* 15:41.
2. *Psalms* 92:1.

forward to serve as his advocate before the Holy One, Blessed is He [after he partook of the Tree of Knowledge and death had been decreed against him]. It [the Sabbath] said: "Master of the Universe: During the six days of Creation no man was punished with death. Must such punishment begin today? Is this my sanctity? Is this my blessing?" In the Sabbath's merit, Adam was spared the judgment of Gehinnom.

Seeing the power of the Sabbath, Adam begin to sing, "A psalm, a song for the seventh day. . ." Said the Sabbath, "You are praising me? Let us both praise the Holy One; it is good to praise Hashem. . ."[1] (*Yalkut Shimoni, Tehillim* §843).

☙ From this *Midrash*, says R' Avraham Pam (*Atarah L'Melech*), we can derive that the sin of causing hurt or distress to one's fellow is especially grave when committed on the Sabbath. Such behavior causes the Sabbath to come forth, as it were, and cry out, "Is this my sanctity? Is this my praise?"

A maidservant in the house of the Chassidic master R' Elimelech of Lizensk recalled, "During the week, angry words were often exchanged among the kitchen staff, as is apt to happen. But every Friday night, something strange would occur. We would embrace one another and say tearfully, 'Forgive me for whatever wrong I may have done during the week. *A gutten Shabbos!*' " Where there exists a true Sabbath spirit, there is no place for pettiness and strife.

R' Shimon bar Yochai alluded to this concept in *Tikkunei Zohar* regarding the verse, "And the Children of Israel shall keep the Sabbath, to make the Sabbath for their generations an eternal covenant."[2] *Tikkunei Zohar* notes that the Torah's spelling of the word לְדֹרֹתָם without any ו (i.e. לְדוֹרוֹתָם) allows for the word to be understood homiletically as if it were vowelized לְדִרָתָם, [*to make the Sabbath*] *for their dwellings.* One should not be satisfied when he experiences an uplift of spirit on the Sabbath; rather, the Sabbath must permeate one's home, and must be evident in the uplifted manner of the entire household.

---

1. *Psalms* 92:2.
2. *Exodus* 31:16.

R' Shimon bar Yochai's students asked him: "Why did the manna not come down for the Israelites once a year [instead of once a day]?"[1] *R' Shimon replied with a parable: "To what is this similar? To the case of a king of flesh and blood who had one son. Once a year, the king would allocate money for sustenance to his son. Consequently, the son would visit his father but once a year. Eventually, the king began to allocate funds on a daily basis, and then the son visited the king daily."*

So too in the case of the Israelites: One who had four or five children would be concerned, "Perhaps the manna will not fall tomorrow and my children will die of starvation!" As a result of such concern, all the Israelites would direct their hearts to their father in Heaven[2] (*Yoma* 76a).

❦ ❦ ❦

The above is illustrated by the following story:

R' Nosson Nota Shapira, famed author of *Megaleh Amukos,* was *Rav* of the city of Cracow in the early part of the seventeenth century. The rabbinate there was a most prestigious position, due to the city's prominence as a bastion of Torah life and scholarship. However, R' Nosson found that the demands of leading such a large community left him little time for pursuing his life's passion, the

1. During their forty-year sojourn in the Wilderness, the Israelites were provided with a daily portion of manna, a food which miraculously fell from Heaven. See *Exodus* Ch. 16.

2. Aside from the reason that they should direct their hearts [לִבָּם] Heavenward, R' Shimon added two more reasons for the manna's falling daily: so that the Jews could partake of it while it was fresh and warm [חַם], and because of the burden of transporting [מַשְׂאוֹי הַדֶּרֶךְ] a year's supply of manna. The first letter of the key word in each of R' Shimon's explanations form the word לֶחֶם, *bread.* Accordingly, when the verse states (*Exodus* 16:4), "I shall rain down for you *bread* [לֶחֶם] from heaven; let the people go out and pick each day's portion on its day," the very word לֶחֶם alludes to the three reasons why the manna was bestowed *each day's portion on its day* — i.e. daily rather than annually (*Ben Yehoyada*).

study of Torah.

When the city of Betchuch approached R' Nosson to become their new rabbi, he eagerly accepted the offer. He was glad to exchange his distinguished office for a lesser one which would leave him more time for studying Torah, and felt certain that his decision to move was correct.

The people of Cracow were devastated when they learned of the imminent departure of their beloved rav. They used whatever powers of persuasion they could muster to convince him to stay, but to no avail. R' Nosson's mind was made up; he was determined to leave.

When the day came and all was in readiness, he prepared to bid farewell to Cracow. Just as the Rav was ready to leave, a man rushed over to him and pleaded, "Please, just come and decide this last *din Torah* (case in a court of Jewish law) before leaving!"

R' Nosson consented and accompanied the man to the *beis din* (court of Jewish law). The two litigants, a businessman and a bagel vendor, each stood ready to present his side.

The businessman began:

"My business requires me to travel often. One day, as I was waiting for a train in the station, I felt very hungry. Looking about, I saw a man —this man! — selling bagels at a stand. I went over to buy a bagel and we got into a discussion regarding whether the correct blessing on the bagel is *hamotzi* or *mezonos*.

"This bagel vendor explained his opinion well, bringing several proofs from the *Shulchan Aruch* (Code of Jewish Law). I was impressed. This man was obviously an accomplished Torah scholar.

"I asked him why a man of his stature was wasting his scholarship selling bagels, and he replied simply, 'What shall I do? I must make a living!'

"I decided to offer him a position. I informed him that I was willing to pay him twice as much as he was currently earning if he would give up his bagel business and spend all his time studying Torah. All I asked in return was that he study with my son every day. This man was delighted with my offer and eagerly accepted.

"Our deal worked out well for both of us for some time. A few weeks later, I had to go on a business trip. Since I would be away for three weeks, I paid the former bagel vendor — now my son's *rebbi* — his wages three weeks in advance.

"Upon my return, I arrived at the train station, very hungry. I thought perhaps someone else now occupied the bagel stand, and I went to look. You can imagine my surprise when I found this 'Torah scholar' — whom I thought I had left teaching my son — manning his stand as before!

" 'What are you doing here?' I shouted at him. 'We made a deal! I paid you wages so that you would spend your days in the study hall, and teach my son, and you let me down!' The bagel seller looked terribly ashamed, but did not explain his actions, and so I have summoned him here," concluded the businessman.

The bagel vendor now began his side of the story.

"Everything this man said is true. I did not keep my promise, and I'm very sorry that I couldn't continue teaching his son. Please let me explain and I'm sure you will understand.

"Things went well for some time: every day I studied Torah and taught the boy, and every week I brought home a salary. But one day, my wife made me realize that things were just not the same. She is a truly G-d-fearing woman, and this is what troubled her:

"When I used to work at the bagel stand, it was very difficult to make ends meet. Every morning before I went out, we would pray to Hashem that I sell sufficient bagels to earn enough to meet our needs for that day.

"Every evening when I came home, my wife would ask me how things went that day. I would answer, 'We must be grateful to Hashem, Who helped me bring home enough money to cover our expenses for today,' and we would thank Hashem for His great kindness. Thus every morning I prayed to Hashem for help, and every evening I thanked Him.

"Each week, my wife would ask whether we would have enough for the coming Shabbos, and again we would pray to Hashem for His help. When I brought home sufficient earnings to purchase our needs for Shabbos, we were full of gratitude to the Al-mighty for His great kindness. All day Shabbos and the next day as well, we would be overjoyed, full of praise to the One Above for the wonderful Shabbos He had enabled us to enjoy.

" 'However,' my wife told me, 'now that you've come home with three weeks' wages in advance, we don't have to pray to Hashem for our livelihood as we used to, and we don't thank Him in the same way. We've begun taking everything for granted! This new position you have taken is driving Hashem from our lives!'

"So, honored Rav, I thought about what my wife said, and realized she is right. I regretted making the change and immediately decided to go back to selling bagels. Of course I never intended to keep this man's money; I will return it."

R' Nosson was astounded at this Jew's words. What faith and purity of heart this couple possessed! He marveled at the holiness of the Jewish nation, and at what special people lived in Cracow. He was so impressed by this incident that he declared, "Bring back my packages! Unload the wagon! I'm not moving to Betchuch after all. I consider it an honor and a privilege to be Rav in a town where there are such people as the bagel vendor and his wife!"[1]

Fear of God

R' Chaninah said in the name of R' Shimon bar Yochai: The Holy One, Blessed is He, has nothing in His treasure house other than a store of the merit of the fear of Heaven, as it is

1. From *"Gut Voch!"* by Avrohom Barash (Mesorah Publications 1998).

stated,[1] *". . .the fear of Hashem, that is His storehouse"* (*Berachos* 34b).

The Scriptural verse cited by R' Shimon begins with an allusion to the Six Orders of the Mishnah, the foundation of Oral Law.[2] In *Nefesh HaChaim,*[3] R' Chaim of Volozhin elaborates:

> Fear of God is the "storehouse" of the wisdom of the holy Torah, for through it the Torah remains with the student. If man does not first prepare the storehouse that is fear of God, then the abundant "grain" that is Torah will be lying out in the field to be trampled. . . for it will not remain with him at all. To the above verse, the *Midrash*[4] states: "You may find a man who studies *Midrash, Halachah* and *Aggadah;* if he does not possess fear of sin, he possesses nothing at all. . ."
>
> To the degree that one prepares his storehouse of fear of God, to that degree will he be able to gather in, safeguard and retain the grain of Torah for his storehouse to hold. . . The hand of God is open, as it were, to grant each one of His treasured people an unceasing flow of wisdom and exceptional depth of understanding, which can remain with him and be inscribed upon his heart, and in which he will delight when he brings it with him to the World of Tranquility. However, all this will depend upon the degree of fear of God that one prepares in advance . . .

A Good Name

R' Shimon said: There are three crowns — the crown of Torah, the crown of priesthood, and the crown of kingship; but the crown of a good name surpasses them all (*Avos* 4:17).

---

1. *Isaiah* 33:6.
2. See *Shabbos* 31a.
3. 4:4-5.
4. *Shemos Rabbah* 30.

R' Shimon bar Yochai also stated: "A good name is more precious than the Holy Ark. While the Holy Ark went only three days' distance before the Israelites in the Wilderness, a man's good name precedes him all over the world."[1]

The crown of a good name is superior even to the crown of Torah, for if a scholar behaves in an improper manner, he profanes God's Name and causes disgrace to the Torah. As the Talmud teaches: "A Jew should study Scripture and Mishnah, serve Torah scholars and deal graciously with his fellow man. Then others will say of him, 'Fortunate is his father who taught him Torah! Fortunate is his teacher who taught him Torah! Woe to those who do not study Torah! He who studies Torah — how pleasant is his behavior and how proper are his deeds.' "[2] The Talmud continues that if one studies Torah but does not deal graciously with others, he causes the Torah to be despised.

Moreover, a refined character is the foundation upon which Torah can be attained and become a part of one's essence. Without proper *midos* (character traits), Torah study will not impact upon the student as it should (*R' Chaim Vital* in *Shaarei Kedushah*).

Hurtful Words

> *R' Yochanan said in the name of R' Shimon bar Yochai:* Ona'as devarim *(Verbal wrongdoing*[3]*) is a greater sin than monetary wrongdoing, for concerning the former the Torah states, "And you shall fear your God,"*[4] *whereas concerning the latter it is not stated "And you shall fear your God"* (*Bava Metzia* 58b).

Sefer Pele Yoetz states:

> *Ona'as devarim* is a greater sin than monetary wrong-doing. Heaven exacts severe retribution for *ona'as devarim*

1. *Koheles Rabbah* 7:3.
2. *Yoma* 86a.
3. I.e., embarrassing, insulting or deceiving someone.
4. *Leviticus* 25:17.

Many transgress this prohibition out of ignorance of its parameters. As a rule, any statement that will cause one's fellow pain is included in *ona'as devarim*. One should bear in mind the Sages' teaching, "That which is hateful to you, do not do to your friend."[1]

When a person defrauds someone monetarily, he does so in spite of the fact that others will, quite possibly, realize what he has done. But when someone inflicts verbal hurt, he can justify it by claiming that he was sincere and meant well. Thus he indicates that he fears public opinion, but not God Who knows the secrets of his heart. This is why *ona'as devarim* is worse than monetary fraud and why the Torah states regarding *ona'as devarim* "And you shall fear your God" (*Maharsha* based on *Rashi* to *Leviticus* 25:17).

Torah and Kindness

R' Yochanan said in the name of Rabbi Shimon bar Yochai: What is the meaning of that which is written: "Praiseworthy are you who sow by all waters, who send forth the feet of the ox and the donkey"?[2] *[This teaches that] whoever engages in studying Torah and bestowing kindness merits the inheritance of two tribes* (*Bava Kamma* 17a).

Sowing is a metaphor for charity and kindness, while *water* symbolizes Torah. The verse is thus interpreted to mean that whoever studies Torah and practices kindness will "set foot" on the territories of the "ox," a metaphor for Joseph,[3] and the "donkey," a metaphor for Yissachar.[4]

The goal of our striving in this world is the perfection of our souls. The *mitzvos* are the means to achieve this goal. There are two *mitzvos* which enable us to emulate God as He relates to us. One is the study of Torah. Through the study of Torah, we attach

1. *Shabbos* 31a.
2. *Isaiah* 32:20.
3. See *Deuteronomy* 33:17.
4. See *Genesis* 49:14.

ourselves to God's mind, as it were, as He created the world. The second is kindness. The basis of all existence is God's desire to perform kindness for His creations. Hence, when we do acts of kindness with a strong desire, we follow in God's footsteps (*R' Zev Leff*).

Attending to Torah Scholars

R' Yochanan taught in the name of R' Shimon bar Yochai: Attending to those who study Torah is greater than its study, as it is written, "Here is Elisha the son of Shafat who poured water on the hands of Elijah."[1] *The verse does not say that Elisha* studied *under Elijah; rather, it says that he* poured water *on his hands. This teaches that attending to a scholar's needs is greater than studying under him* (*Berachos* 7b).

Attending, in this context, means for the student to take note of the teacher's behavior and learn from it. In the Talmud we find incidents of students who went to great lengths to observe the ways of their teachers. They explained themselves by saying: "This is Torah — it needs to be studied."[2] This method of learning becomes embedded in the heart of the observer and is more effective than listening to the teacher's lectures (*Vilna Gaon* cited by *Maharitz Chayos*).[3]

A Royal Table

R' Shimon says: If three have eaten at the same table and have not spoken words of Torah there, it is as if they have

---

1. *II Kings* 3:11.

2. See *Berachos* 62a.

3. In *Mishnah Succah* (2:1), R' Shimon bar Yochai cites a casual remark of R' Gamliel and derives a law from it. R' Shimon prefaces his derivation with the words: וּלְפִי דַּרְכֵּנוּ לָמַדְנוּ, *and in accordance with our way we learn [from this remark]. Midos Rashbi* writes that the "way" to which R' Shimon refers was his practice of learning not only from the formal lectures of Torah scholars but from their actions and casual remarks as well.

eaten of offerings to the dead idols, as it is said: "For all tables are full of vomit and filth, without the Omnipresent."[1] *But if three have eaten at the same table and have spoken words of Torah there, it is as if they have eaten from the table of the Omnipresent, as it is said: "And he said to me, 'This is the table that is before Hashem.'"*[2] (*Avos* 3:4).

⁂ According to most religious philosophies, there is a dichotomy between the physical and the spiritual. They consider man to be basically a sensual being, who achieves a degree of spirituality only when he is involved in "religious" activities such as prayer or ritual, but never achieves peaceful coexistence between his body and his spirit.

Judaism views the matter in exactly the opposite way. Not only is physical existence impossible without the satisfaction of spiritual needs, but spirituality must be realized through physical vehicles. Spiritual ideas must assume concrete forms. Man is a physical being elevated by the soul God blew into him.[3]

One who engages in a physical act of eating without introducing a spiritual element into his meal establishes a demarcation between the physical and spiritual domains; in effect, he is declaring that they share no interaction. His meal is therefore equivalent to an offering brought before an idol. Conversely, people who follow the Torah's view of life by giving physical garb to spiritual concepts, and by elevating the physical with an infusion of spirituality, eat from God's table (R' Yaakov Kamenetsky in *Emes L'Yaakov*).

---

1. *Isaiah* 28:8.

2. *Ezekiel* 41:22. According to *Rav* and *Rashi,* one can fulfill the obligation to recite words of Torah at the table by reciting *Bircas HaMazon* which contains many Scriptural verses. Nonetheless, it is laudatory not to rely on this, but instead to engage in study or Torah-oriented conversation (see *Tosafos Yom Tov* ad loc. and *Magen Avraham, Orach Chaim* 170).

Sfas Emes suggests that while recitation of *Bircas HaMazon* elevates the meal above the level of *offerings to the dead idols,* only actual discussion of Torah will raise it to the level where it is considered *God's table.*

3. See *Genesis* 2:7.

God's Presence in Our Midst

> *R' Shimon bar Yochai said: Take note of how beloved are the Children of Israel before the Holy One, Blessed is He. For wherever they were exiled, the Shechinah (Divine Presence) was with them. When they were exiled to Egypt, the Shechinah was with them, as it is said, "Was I not revealed to your father's house when they were in Egypt. . .?"*[1]
>
> *When they were exiled to Babylon, the Shechinah was with them, as it is said, "For your sake have I been sent to Babylon."*[2] *And also at the time when they are destined to be redeemed, the Shechinah will be with them, as it is said, "And Hashem will return with your returning exiles."*[3] *The verse does not states, "He will bring back," but "He will return."*[4] *This teaches that the Holy One, Blessed is He, will return with them from the exiles* (*Megillah* 29a).

God is, of course, Omnipresent. Nevertheless, there are places where His Presence is made apparent — where the *Shechinah* reveals itself, as it were. R' Shimon bar Yochai teaches that the *Shechinah* reveals itself in exile as well (*Maharsha*).

The *Shechinah* is manifest whenever a *minyan* (quorum) of Jews gather in prayer. *Maharal* writes:

> . . . the *Shechinah* is with Israel in exile . . . and when they gather together . . . as for example, during communal prayer, that is considered an "ingathering" of the dispersion which is Israel's lot among the nations, and it can be viewed as a redemption from among the nations.[5]

The halls of Torah study also serve as an abode in exile for the *Shechinah*. In fact, after citing this teaching of R' Shimon, the Talmud states that when the prophet Ezekiel spoke of a מִקְדָּשׁ

---

1. *I Samuel* 2:27.
2. *Isaiah* 43:14.
3. *Deuteronomy* 30:3.
4. The verse reads וְשָׁב rather than וְהֵשִׁיב.
5. *Ohr Chadash* 4:16.

מְעַט, *small sanctuary,* in exile,[1] he was referring to the synagogues and study halls.

R' Chaim of Volozhin wrote:

> Since the Destruction of our Temple when the children were banished from the table of their Father, the *Shechinah* moves about, as it were, for it can find no rest. *And there is nothing left but this Torah.*[2] When the holy nation of Israel discusses and delves into Torah properly, they become a miniature sanctuary for the *Shechinah*. . .[3]

Elsewhere, R' Chaim expounds upon this last point:

> If man will sanctify himself appropriately through observance of all the *mitzvos* . . . then he is a Temple — literally — and the *Shechinah* rests within him; as it is written, "The sanctuary of Hashem are they."[4]

Finally, the Jewish home is referred to by our Sages as a מִקְדָּשׁ מְעַט, *small sanctuary.* According to *Ramban,*[5] the *Mishkan* (Tabernacle) was meant to be a replica of the tent of the matriarch Sarah — the prototype Jewish home! A Jewish home can be imbued with God's holiness — if its inhabitants will allow it to enter.

A Jew's Worth

> *R' Shimon bar Yochai said: From where do we know that if Israel had been missing even one man, the Divine Presence would not have revealed itself to them [to give them the Torah]? For it is written, ". . .for on the third day, Hashem shall descend in the sight of the entire people at Mount Sinai"*[6] (*Devarim Rabbah* 7:8).

---

1. *Ezekiel* 11:16.
2. From the Yom Kippur *Ne'ilah* service.
3. *Nefesh HaChaim* 4:34.
4. Ibid. 1:4; see footnote there.
5. Introduction to the Book of *Exodus.*
6. *Exodus* 19:11.

ও R' Chaim Shmulevitz (*Sichos Mussar*) writes that the level of a generation's attachment to and achievements in Torah is in direct proportion to the degree of harmony that prevails among the Jews at that time.[1]

At Sinai, the Jews were "like one man with one heart."[2] But the Revelation required more than a unity of spirit. Had a single Jew been absent, the Jews' acceptance of the Torah would have been lacking, for the "soul" that is the nation of Israel would not have been fully present.

Peace Is Precious

Rabbi Shimon bar Yochai said: Peace is precious, for all blessings are encompassed by it, as it is written, "Hashem will give might to his people, Hashem will bless His people with peace"[3] (*Vayikra Rabbah* 9:5).

ও The verse states that God will bless Israel בַּשָּׁלוֹם which can be translated *in peace*. With his statement, R' Shimon bar Yochai alludes to the teaching that, "The Holy One, Blessed is He, did not find a vessel which can contain blessing, other than [the vessel of] peace."[4]

Shalom bayis, harmony in the home, is the "vessel" which holds the blessings for which every Jew should yearn. R' Avraham Pam (*Atarah L'Melech*) notes that because *shalom bayis* is so crucial, it needs constant attention and reinforcement. We see this in the Torah, regarding the marriage of Abraham and Sarah, which surely was one of harmony. Abraham and Sarah were

1. Thus do the Sages teach that at the time when the Purim miracle occurred, the Jews reaffirmed their acceptance of the Torah on a level that surpassed their acceptance at Sinai (*Shabbos* 88a). The decree of genocide issued by Haman caused all barriers among Jews to crumble. The nation that Haman had described as "scattered and dispersed" (*Esther* 3:8) had become unified as never before.

2. *Rashi* to *Exodus* 19:2, citing *Mechilta.* For an additional insight into the significance of every Jew's witnessing the Revelation, see *Maharsha* to *Berachos* 58a, s.v. חכם הרזים.

3. *Psalms* 29:11.

4. *Mishnah Uketzin* 3:12.

ninety-nine and eighty-nine, respectively, when three angels, disguised as wayfarers, visited them. They inquired of Abraham, "Where is Sarah your wife?" though they knew that she was in her tent. They did this, say the Sages, to emphasize her modesty "in order to endear her to her husband."[1]

Aggadic Accounts

The Message of the Dove

Zohar Chadash[2] provides the following supplement to the account of R' Shimon bar Yochai's years in the cave recorded in Tractate *Shabbos.*[3]

> Once, the Sages were discussing a distinction between the *Tochachah* (Admonition) of *Leviticus*[4] and the *Tochachah* of *Deuteronomy.*[5] The former, which predicts the sufferings at the time of the First Destruction,[6] contains verses of consolation,[7] while the latter, which predicts the sufferings during and after the Second Destruction, contains no consolation. The Sages did not know why this was so.
>
> R' Yehudah bar Ilai arose and said, "Woe that Bar

---

1. *Bava Metzia* 87a.

2. *Parashas Ki Savo.*

3. See p. 45.

4. *Leviticus* 26:14-43.

5. *Deuteronomy* 28:15-68.

6. See *Ramban* to *Leviticus* 26:16.

7. "I will remember My covenant with Jacob and also My covenant with Isaac, and also My covenant with Abraham will I remember, and I will remember the Land" (Leviticus 26:42); and "But despite all this, while they are in the land of their enemies, I will not have been abhorred by them nor will I have rejected them to obliterate them, to annul My covenant with them — for I am Hashem, their God" (ibid. 44).

Yochai is not with us, and there is no one who knows his whereabouts! And if someone would know his whereabouts, he would not be permitted to reveal it."[1]

One morning, R' Yose bar Yehudah watched a group of birds in flight. A lone dove trailed behind the flock. R' Yose arose and said, "O dove, O dove, you who are trustworthy since the days of the Flood,[2] and to whom Israel is likened[3] — to you praise is due, to you praise is fitting! Go and fulfill a mission for me to the place where Bar Yochai is found."

The dove circled and landed before him. R' Yose wrote a note which the dove took in its mouth and brought to R' Shimon in the cave where he was hiding. R' Shimon and his son R' Elazar read the note and wept. Said R' Shimon, "I am weeping that I have been separated from my colleagues and I am weeping over these matters [i.e., the answer to their question] which have not been revealed to them. And what shall the later generations do when they will ponder this?"[4]

No sooner had R' Shimon said these words than Elijah the Prophet appeared to him and revealed the secret of this matter: All the promises and consolations regarding the end of this Exile are hidden in the words of the second *Tochachah.*[5] Moreover, "the verses of the curses which foretell the worst punishments contain the revelation of the Redemption — and all is contingent on *teshuvah* (repentance)."

In the evening, R' Shimon wrote this down on a paper and placed it in the dove's mouth. The dove returned to R' Yose who was waiting at the very spot from which the dove had departed. When R' Yose spotted the bird, he exclaimed, "O dove! How trustworthy are you, more than

---

1. Lest this information become known to the Roman government.

2. *Genesis* 8:8-12.

3. *Zohar,* Vol. I, 215b.

4. The fact that the second *Tochachah* contains no consolation might cause the people to grow despondent.

5. In *Zohar* (ad loc.) illustrations of this are given.

any other bird beneath the heavens!" He took the note, went to his colleagues and related to them what had transpired.

R' Yehudah wept and exclaimed, "Woe! Though we do not know his [R' Shimon's] whereabouts, *wherever the tree falls, there it remains*[1] — the place where Bar Yochai is, his colleagues are with him and are inspired by him. Praiseworthy is the soul of Bar Yochai, for the Holy One, Blessed is He, performs miracles for him. Bar Yochai decrees, and the Holy One, Blessed is He, upholds his decree."[2]

Of Marriage and Blessing

In the city of Sidon, there was a couple who remained childless after ten years of marriage. They came before R' Shimon bar Yochai to request that he arrange their divorce. R' Shimon told them: "By your lives, just as your wedding was celebrated with food and drink, so too should you part from one another with food and drink."

The couple obeyed these instructions and made a holiday for themselves, highlighted by a huge feast. And what did the wife do at this feast? She served her husband an abundance of wine until he became drunk. In his inebriated state, he told his wife, "My daughter, pick any good object that you see in the house and take it with you when you return to your father!"

What did the woman do? When her husband was sound asleep, she instructed her servants, "Lift up his bed and bring him to my father's house!" In the middle of the night, the husband awoke, the effects of the wine having worn off. "My daughter," he asked his wife, "where am I?"

"In my father's house," the wife replied.

"But why?" he asked.

1. *Ecclesiastes* 11:3.

2. See *Shabbos* 59b; see also p. 172.

"Did you not tell me in the evening that I could choose any good object in your house and take it to my father's house? I have nothing better in this world than you!"

The two returned to R' Shimon bar Yochai. He prayed for them and they were blessed with a child. This teaches that just as the Holy One, Blessed is He, grants children to the barren, so too do the righteous grant children to the barren through their prayers (*Shir HaShirim Rabbah* 1:3).

ঌ R' Chaim Shmulevitz asked: What was R' Shimon bar Yochai's intention when he told the couple to celebrate their parting as they had celebrated their wedding day? He explained that it was R' Shimon's hope that the couple, through their celebrating together, would awaken the feelings which they had felt for one another on their wedding day. If they would succeed, then their love for one another would not allow them to part, though they remained childless. They succeeded at this, and as a result, made themselves worthy of blessing.

Bar Mitzvah

ঌ In *Zohar,* we find a number of statements regarding the spiritual milestone of becoming a bar mitzvah:

R' Elazar said: Until thirteen years, man struggles with the physical components of his soul; after that time, if he wishes to be a righteous person, he will be given a spiritually elevated soul drawn from beneath the throne of the Heavenly King (*Zohar Chadash, Genesis*).

The fruits of a tree in its first three years are deemed *orlah* (closed off) and are forbidden.[1] In a similar sense, the first thirteen years of a boy's life are considered *orlah,* spiritually underdeveloped. After that time, his soul is aroused to pursue elevated service to God, to prevent his physical desires from overtaking him (*Zohar Chadash, Genesis* 14a).

1. See *Leviticus* 19:23.

In *Zohar Chadash,* we find an account of the day when R' Elazar, son of R' Shimon, became a bar mitzvah:

> It happened that R' Shimon bar Yochai invited the Sages of the Mishnah to partake of a lavish meal which he had prepared for them. The entire house was decorated with precious vessels. He seated the Sages to one side while he sat on the other side. They asked him, "What is the source of our master's gladness on this day, that it is greater than on other days?"
>
> R' Shimon replied, "On this day, an exalted, sanctified soul descended to R' Elazar my son, and with this feast, my joy is complete." R' Shimon seated his son R' Elazar next to him and said, "Be seated, my son. . . for on this day you are sanctified among the lot of the sanctified" (*Zohar Chadash, Midrash HaNe'elam* 10b).

Spending Wisely

The Talmud teaches:[1]

> R' Yehudah the son of R' Shalom expounded: Just as a person's sustenance [for the coming year] is apportioned for him from Rosh Hashanah, so a person's losses [for the coming year] are apportioned for him from Rosh Hashanah. If one merited [good fortune, he will give the amount he must lose to the poor, in compliance with the verse,] " You will break your bread for the hungry."[2] But if he did not merit [good fortune, then that amount will be confiscated from him, in fulfillment of the verse,] ". . . and wailing poor you will bring to the house."[3]

This concept is illustrated by the following *Midrash*:

> On the night of Rosh Hashanah, it was shown to R'

1. *Bava Basra* 10a.

2. *Isaiah* 58:7.

3. Ibid. Earlier, the Talmud interpreted *wailing poor* as a reference to the Roman government, which constantly bemoaned lack of funds and taxed its subject nations accordingly.

Shimon bar Yochai in a dream that in the coming year, his nephews would be fined 600 *dinarim*[1] by the ruling government. R' Shimon prevailed upon his nephews to become administrators of a charity fund for the poor [but did not inform them of his dream]. They asked R' Shimon: "From where shall we procure the funds?" He told them: "Distribute funds from your own resources and keep a record of it all. At year's end, if you have suffered any losses, I will make it up to you."

As the year drew to a close, someone slandered them before the government with regard to their silk dealings. One day, as they were involved with their silk work, a government officer appeared and issued an ultimatum: "Either you will make the king a silk robe free of charge, or you will have to pay a fine of six hundred *dinarim.*" He then arrested them and had them imprisoned.

Upon learning of what had transpired, R' Shimon visited his nephews in prison. He asked them, "How much money have you distributed to the poor this year?" They responded by showing him the record of the year's distributions. R' Shimon calculated the total to be 594 *dinarim.* He told his nephews: "Give me 6 *dinarim* and I will have you freed from prison." His nephews were incredulous. "The officer demanded of us 600 *dinarim* and you say that with *six dinarim* you can have us freed?" R' Shimon responded, "Give me six *dinarim* and you will not have to bother with them." They handed over six *dinarim,* which R' Shimon offered as a bribe to the officer who had ordered their imprisonment. The officer accepted the bribe, agreed to say nothing to the king, and freed them.

R' Shimon's nephews said to him, "Did you in fact know that we were going to be fined this amount [which is why you only asked us for six *dinarim*]?" R' Shimon replied, "By your lives, since the night of Rosh Hashanah, I have known that it was decreed that you should pay six hundred *dinarim* to the king."

---

1. A silver coin. The silver content of the coin was equal to ninety-six grains of barley. It was worth 1/24 the value of a gold *dinar.*

R' Shimon's nephews did not understand why he had not informed them of this from the start. "Had you told us of this, would we not have given six hundred *dinarim* for the *mitzvah* [of assisting the poor]? [The poor would have benefited and we would have been saved so much pain and distress!]"[1]

R' Shimon replied, "Certainly you would have done so. However, I wanted you to do the *mitzvah* for its own sake [with pure intentions, not in order to escape the decree]" (*Vayikra Rabbah* 34:12).[2]

A Gift from Above

☙ *Zohar* teaches that when a person finds himself in a dangerous situation, Heaven sometimes sends him a "gift" in the form of a poor person whom he can assist with *tzedakah,* so that the merit of this great *mitzvah* will stand by him in his hour of need.

One day, R' Yitzchak, a disciple of R' Shimon bar Yochai, was met by a poor man whose purse was empty, save for half a *ma'ah* (a small coin). The man pleaded with R' Yitzchak to have mercy on him and his family. R' Yitzchak replied that his financial situation was precarious as well; he, too, had but half a *ma'ah* on his person. The poor man persisted that were R' Yitzchak to give him this coin, he would then have a full *ma'ah* to buy food for his family. R' Yitzchak handed the man his coin and the two parted.

That night, R' Yitzchak dreamt that he was standing by the seashore when bandits descended upon him and sought to cast him into the ocean. Suddenly, R' Yitzchak saw his teacher, R' Shimon bar Yochai, extending his hand to rescue him. R' Yitzchak reached towards R' Shimon — but the distance was too great.

Then the poor man suddenly appeared, and bridged the

1. Though R' Shimon had promised that he would reimburse them for any losses they might suffer, they still gave *tzedakah* to the poor with the intention of helping their needy brethren, and not because they wanted to avoid problems with the government (*Midrash Rabbah HaMevuar*).

2. See *Bava Basra* 10a where an almost identical story is told about Rabban Yochanan ben Zakai.

gap between R' Shimon and R' Yitzchak. He placed R' Yitzchak's hand in that of his teacher and disappeared.

When R' Yitzchak awoke, he extemporaneously uttered the verse, "Praiseworthy is he who contemplates the needy; on the day of disaster, Hashem will rescue him."[1] His charity had earned him the merit of R' Shimon bar Yochai's prayers on his behalf.

More Precious than Gold

It happened that a student of R' Shimon bar Yochai journeyed to another land and returned to Israel a wealthy man. Taking note of this, other students became envious and desired to journey to other lands as well.

R' Shimon learned of this and took his students to a valley near the entrance to Meron.[2] He prayed: "Valley, valley, become filled with *dinarim* of gold!" The valley began to flow with *dinarim*.

R' Shimon turned to his students and said: "If it is gold that you seek — here is gold! Take what you want. Realize, however, that whoever takes now is taking [from] his share in the World to Come, for the reward of Torah is [reserved] only for the World to Come.[3] [They withdrew their hands from taking anything.[4]] This is the intent of, "She joyfully awaits the very last day"[5] (*Shemos Rabbah* 52:2).

☙ In *Midrash Shochar Tov,* the story concludes with the students exclaiming: "For You have gladdened me, Hashem, with Your deeds; at the works of Your hands I will sing glad song."[6]

---

1. *Psalms* 41:2.

2. From *Idra Zuta* it appears that R' Shimon actually resided near Meron. To this day, there is a remnant at the mountain top in Meron of a huge edifice with a beautiful archway. It is said that this was the *Beis HaKnesses D'Rashbi* (Synagogue of R' Shimon bar Yochai — from *Midos Rashbi*).

3. That is, the principal reward. The "fruits," however, are enjoyed in this world. See *Mishnah Pe'ah* 1:1.

4. This appears in the version of *Midrash Shochar Tov*.

5. *Proverbs* 31:25. The faithful Jew may endure difficulties in this world, but he will "smile" when at his life's end he reaps the rewards of his efforts.

6. *Psalms* 92:5.

R' Asher Zelig Margulies explains this with a story which he heard from his teacher, R' Uri Strelisker of Jerusalem, a grandson of the Chassidic master R' Uri, the *Saraph* (Fiery One) of Strelisk:

Once, R' Uri's disciples found themselves suffering the pangs of poverty. They wanted desperately to discuss their situation with their master and teacher, but none of them had the courage to broach the subject. R' Uri was totally removed from earthly wants; would he not be displeased to hear them complaining about their material situation?

One of them hit upon an idea. He told his fellow disciples, "I will approach the *Rebbe* with our problem, but I will do it in the morning before *Shacharis.* And I want all of you to be there with me."

The next morning, the disciples entered the *Saraph's* study as he prepared to pray. "What is it that requires my attention before *davening* (praying)?" he asked.

His disciple stepped forward. "*Rebbe,*" he began, "we are about to recite *Birchos HaShachar* (Morning Blessings) in which we praise God *Who has provided me my every need. Rebbe,* we all lack the most basic needs — we barely have bread to eat and our clothing are threadbare. How can we recite this blessing with true feeling?"

R' Uri smiled and replied, "You must believe with perfect faith that if this is the situation into which God has placed you, then this *is* what you need at this time!"[1]

Similarly, R' Shimon bar Yochai taught his students that their lack of wealth was actually their greatest benefit, for in this way the reward of their Torah study would be stored away for the Next World. Realizing this, his students responded, "For You have gladdened me, Hashem, with Your deeds; at the works of Your hands I will sing glad song."

---

1. R' Avraham Pam relates a similar story: There was a Jew who, in spite of his having lived his entire life in dire poverty, remained steadfast in his faith, and prayed with intense concentration. Someone once overheard this man reciting the morning blessing, "Blessed are You. . . Who has provided me my every need," with great joy.

Asked the passerby, "Can you really say that your every need has been provided for? You are among the poorest of the poor!"

The man replied: "Can one really know, on his own, what his particular needs are? If God has made me poor, then obviously this condition is necessary for me to fulfill my purpose in life. Poverty is what my soul needs, and I have been granted this need in full measure!"

Lag BaOmer Stories

R' Shimon's Power (I)

⇜§ In the year 5660 (1900), a Jew named R' Ozer Razin journeyed from Riga, Latvia to Jerusalem, bringing with him his young son Shmuel. Shmuel was a child who possessed great spiritual ambition and R' Ozer was convinced that his potential could best be fulfilled by his spending the years of his youth in the rarefied atmosphere of the Holy City where his uncle, R' Yedidyah Grodner, resided. R' Yedidyah combined Torah scholarship with devotion to prayer and other areas of observance. He was a regular at the Tifereth Yisrael *minyan,* which recited the morning *Shemoneh Esrei* each morning at sunrise (the most preferred time). R' Yedidyah readily welcomed his nephew to his home, where he and his wife treated Shmuel like a son.

R' Yedidyah and his wife grew deeply attached to the boy. They enrolled him at the Eitz Chaim Yeshivah, from which blossomed forth many of the great Torah personalities of the next generation. In addition, R' Yedidyah studied with Shmuel privately for an hour a day and also hired a tutor to sharpen the boy's learning skills.

In one of his letters home, Shmuel wrote:

> I have now completed *Mesilas Yesharim* [1] for the first time and I feel as if I have been transformed into a different person. When Uncle Yedidyah learns *Mesilas Yesharim* with me, tears stream down his cheeks. He told me that many of the Jews here in the Old City are "living *Mesilas Yesharims.*" My dream is to be like them . . .

Two years after Shmuel's arrival in Jerusalem, tragedy struck. He became afflicted with a mysterious eye disease which caused his eyesight to grow steadily weaker as time passed. Doctors could not identify the cause of the illness and were at a loss to prescribe medication. They predicted that at the present rate of deterioration, it would not be long before young Shmuel was completely blind.

---

1. The classic ethical work by Rabbi Moshe Chaim Luzzato (*Ramchal*).

R' Yedidyah and his wife were overcome with anguish. They hurried in vain from doctor to doctor hoping to find a cure. They prayed and distributed *tzedakah* as a source of merit for Shmuel's recovery.

As time passed and the situation worsened, R' Yedidyah took to rising at midnight and would remain awake the remainder of the night praying tearfully. At dawn, he would make his way to the Western Wall and continue to pray that his nephew, who had shown such promise, be granted his full eyesight once again.

One winter evening, the dreaded moment arrived. As Shmuel sat learning with his private tutor, R' David Lebel, he was suddenly plunged into darkness. He had become totally blind.

Amazingly, Shmuel retained his composure at that tragic moment. After telling his tutor what had happened, he said, "Please say the words slowly from now on and I will repeat them after you, word by word."

Meanwhile, Shmuel's aunt ran from the house and summoned the neighbors. One of them brought to the house Professor Sukmeinski, a renowned ophthalmologist who had been sent to Jerusalem by Baron Rothschild to help curb the rash of eye-related ailments which were plaguing the city's residents. After examining Shmuel, the Professor ruled out surgery and declared that there was yet a very slim chance that the boy's eyesight would return. There was nothing left to do but pray.

Days passed with no improvement. At night, R' Yedidyah and his wife would listen as Shmuel would recite the bedtime *Shema* and then utter his own prayer: "Master of the Universe: Is it for earthly pleasures or treats that I am asking? All that I desire is that my eyes be illuminated by the light of Your holy Torah. Please, Hashem, heal my eyes so that I may once again see the written word and study it without impediment."

Two weeks passed with no change in Shmuel's condition. R' Yedidyah felt that his nephew was in desperate need of a change of routine, so he arranged for the boy to spend some time at the home of R' Shimon Hausman in Hebron. R' Shimon was a highly regarded communal activist, a kindhearted man who never tired of serving his brethren. R' Shimon welcomed R' Yedidyah and Shmuel into his home and his heart melted with compassion upon hearing of the boy's plight. He readily agreed to take the boy under his charge for an unlimited amount of time.

In those days, the city of Hebron was led by two towering Torah personalities. R' Shimon Menasheh Chaikan, a renowned kabbalist, was the city's Ashkenazic *Rav,* while its Sephardic community was led by R' Chaim Chizkiyahu Medini, author of *Sdei Chemed.* A close relationship existed between these two *tzaddikim* and it was known that they met together somewhere in the city each night. It was said that at midnight, the two prayed together at a holy site, possibly the Tomb of the Patriarchs, for the abolishment of harsh decrees.

One day, R' Shimon Hausman was struck by an idea. Perhaps, if he would go with Shmuel in the darkness of night and meet these two *tzaddikim,* they would bestow their blessing that the child's eyesight be restored. Exactly what these two kabbalists did together each night and where they met was a secret known to no one but themselves. To confront them during their nightly meeting might be overstepping the bounds of propriety and could possibly invoke their indignation. Therefore, the thought of implementing this plan filled R' Shimon with dread, but he was willing to take the risk for Shmuel's sake.

Night after night, R' Shimon, his hand firmly clenching that of Shmuel, took to walking near the homes of the two *rabbanim.* Finally, one night as R' Shimon and Shmuel were standing near the courtyard of R' Shimon Menasheh's house, the door swung open and the two *rabbanim* emerged.

R' Shimon Hausman approached and, trembling with fear, he placed the boy squarely between the two *tzaddikim.* He then disappeared into the darkness without offering a word of explanation. His actions were, indeed, correct; no explanation was necessary. The *tzaddikim* immediately sensed the child's predicament. R' Shimon Menashe grasped Shmuel's right hand, the *Sdei Chemed* his left, and the three began to walk together in the darkness.

Shmuel related the details of his woeful tale. When he had finished, the *Sdei Chemed* asked him, "What were the last words that you learned before the moment when you could no longer see?"

"I was studying *Masechta Chullin,*" the boy replied, "and the last words that I read were: אָנוּ עַל מִי נִסְמוֹךְ? בֹּאוּ וְנִסְמוֹךְ עַל דִּבְרֵי רַבִּי שִׁמְעוֹן, *Upon whom are we to rely? Come, let us rely upon the words of Rabbi Shimon.*"[1]

"That is your solution!" the two *tzaddikim* exclaimed. "You must go to Meron to the tomb of Rabbi Shimon bar Yochai, upon whose merit you can surely rely! Go there and pray that in R' Shimon's merit, Hashem should heal you."

The next morning, R' Shimon brought Shmuel back home to his uncle in Jerusalem and soon after, R' Yedidyah and his nephew set out by donkey for Meron. The trip in those days, over rugged terrain, was a difficult one for anyone, even more so for a middle-aged man leading a young blind boy. But nothing could prevent them from reaching their destination. They arrived at the tomb of Rabbi Shimon and entered the *beis midrash* at the site, with the intention of not leaving the area until their prayers were answered.

Day after day, the two remained there, their every waking moment dedicated either to heartfelt prayer or intensive study. On the fifth day, as they prepared to recite the Book of *Psalms* with Shmuel repeating after R' Yedidyah word by word, the boy suddenly exclaimed, "Uncle — I can see the outline of your body! I can see the outline of the objects near you!" Indeed, his eyesight had begun to return.

They remained there a total of thirteen days, until Shmuel's eyesight was fully restored. On that day, the two held hands in an ecstatic dance, as they sang the Lag BaOmer song of R' Shimon's praises, *"Va'amartem Ko Lechoi,"*[2] which concludes with:

> *May His Torah shield us, it is the light of our eyes, he will intercede for good on our behalf — our master, Bar Yochai!*

And they added a stanza of their own:

> *Upon whom can we rely? Come, let us rely upon Rabbi Shimon bar Yochai!*[3]

---

1. *Chullin* 36a.

2. The song is found on p. 168.

3. This story appears in *Yerushalayim shel Maalah* (The Heavenly City) by Menachem Gerlitz.

R' Shimon's Power (II)

In his work, *Hilula D'Rashbi,* the noted kabbalist R' Asher Zelig Margulies wrote the following:

> While this work is not one of stories, nevertheless, I cannot restrain myself from relating the workings of Hashem, an awesome story of a wondrous miracle which we witnessed with our own eyes. Behold! I am an eyewitness to this miracle which took place in Meron on Lag BaOmer in the year 5683 (1923).

The following is a translation of R' Margulies' account:

That year, Lag BaOmer fell on a Friday. Most of the multitudes who had come there for Lag BaOmer remained there for the Sabbath — we experienced a Sabbath gladness that was exalted and wondrous.

It happened on Sabbath morning, after the last *minyan* had completed the *Mussaf* prayer at around noon in the study hall at the tomb of *Rashbi.* Suddenly, we heard a great, anguished cry. A Sefardic woman had brought her three-year-old boy to fulfill her vow — a well-known custom — that his *chalakah* (first haircut) would take place at R' Shimon's tomb. Then without warning, the boy was struck with cholera and died at the tomb. The child was placed in a small room on the roof of the building which stands above the tomb, while doctors on the scene ordered that everyone present be quarantined. People began to panic and some attempted to leave, but police soon arrived and sealed off the area.

Piercing cries and wailing filled the air; above them all, the anguished cry of the young mother whose one and only child had died on the day after his *chalakah* had been celebrated with such joy. I personally saw the lifeless body of the boy, his facial appearance drained of all color.

The entire assemblage was pained beyond description; we simply found it impossible to recite *Kiddush* and partake of the Sabbath morning meal. Then suddenly, the mother of the child, in the way of Jewish women of valor, girded herself with great inner strength. She went to the room where her son lay, lifted him up into her arms and carried him downstairs to the synagogue which is at the tomb of R' Shimon. She placed the body on the floor and then, in an anguished, tear-choked voice, she cried out:

> O *tzaddik,* O *tzaddik, tzaddik* Rabbi Shimon! Behold! I, your maidservant, came here in your honor, to cut the hair of my only child, whom God granted to me in your merit. I fulfilled my vow that I would bring him here [for his first haircut] on Lag BaOmer. Yesterday, I brought him here alive, and had his hair cut accompanied by music, song, food and drink, and much joy. Now, how can I leave from here without my child? How will I enter my house . . . ?

Her cries and wailing could be heard throught the area — whose heart could not be melted, hearing such anguished cries of inner pain?

The woman then stood up and said:

> *Tzaddik, tzaddik!* I am leaving my child before you as he is. I beg of you, do not shame me, do not turn me away empty-handed. Return my child to me alive and well as he was when I brought him before you. Let the Name of God, as well as your name, be sanctified in the world, and let it be known that there is a God Who rules this world, and there are *tzaddikim* whose bidding He fulfills.

As a *segulah* (auspicious omen), they closed the doors of the synagogue, leaving the child inside alone. After a few moments, the sounds of the boy crying for his mother could be heard coming from the synagogue. The *chacham* (Sefardic scholar) who was there opened the door for the mother to enter. The little boy, who was now standing on his feet, cried, "*Ima* (Mother), give me some water, for I am thirsty." They brought him some water, after which his mother carried him upstairs to the room where he had been previously.

A great tumult erupted as news spread that the child had returned to life. The entire assemblage came to see with their own eyes, and the doctors gathered to examine the child. They admitted that by the laws of nature, the impossible had occurred.

It could only have been a miracle, in the merit of the holy *Tanna,* Rabbi Shimon bar Yochai. The quarantine was lifted.

The *kiddush Hashem* (sanctification of God's Name) was incredible. The entire assemblage recited the blessing of *[Blessed are You, Hashem . . .] Who resuscitates the dead.*[1]

R' Shimon's Power (III)

The following is adapted from an article by Baruch Ben Zahav which appeared in **Hamodia**. *It is written in the first person as it appeared there.*

We were a group of young men rejoicing together on the night of Lag BaOmer. Caught up in the holy spirit of the day, we began to recount the power of Rabbi Shimon bar Yochai, during his lifetime and throughout the generations.

Someone mentioned the *segulah* (auspicious omen) mentioned in *Taamei HaMinhagim* to pray at the grave of R' Shimon on behalf of a childless couple and promise that, if the couple will be granted a child within the coming year, then on Lag BaOmer of that year 18 *roytel* (approximately 53 liters) of wine will be distributed in Meron to those who come to pray on R' Shimon's *hilula.*

One of the young men present mentioned that on the previous Lag BaOmer, a friend of his had made such a promise on behalf of a couple who had been childless for many years. The couple had been blessed with a child and their friend was planning to distribute 18 *roytels* of grape juice at Meron in the morning.

I thought of a close friend of mine who was childless after six years of marriage. I stood up and announced, "I accept upon myself *b'li neder* (without the force of a vow) to distribute 18 *roytels* of grape juice in Meron on Lag BaOmer 5757 (1997) if . . . [2] will be granted a child within the year."

---

1. *Shaar Yissoschor* writes that the *gematria* (numerical value) of שִׁמְעוֹן בֶּן יוֹחָאי is equal to that of מְחַיֵּה מֵתִים, *one who resucitates the dead* (553).

2. At this point, one inserts פלוני בן פלונית, the husband's Hebrew name, *son of* his mother's Hebrew name. The wife's Hebrew name [*daughter of* her mother's Hebrew name] should be said as well.

No sooner had I said these words than another man stood up and uttered the same resolution on behalf of a friend.

We drank *"L'chayim"* and wished one another *"Mazel tov."* The next morning at Meron, we repeated our promises.

☙ The Case of the Forgotten Cases

One month before Lag BaOmer 5757, my friend and his wife celebrated the *bris* of their newborn son. Two weeks later, the other couple on whose behalf a promise had been uttered were also blessed with a child.

The man who had made his promise on behalf of the second couple was a friend of mine and lives in my neighborhood. Happily, we made plans to transport 106 liters of grape juice to Meron in honor of Lag BaOmer to fulfill our promises. Accomplishing this should not have been very difficult; on Lag BaOmer, buses with large luggage compartments would be leaving from our neighborhood in Ashdod for Meron. However, my friend and I agreed to use another means of transport which would be more difficult and more expensive — but did have one advantage. A charity organization in Bnei Brak charges a fee to deliver such *"segulah"* beverages to the tomb of R' Shimon in honor of Lag BaOmer, and also undertakes to distribute the drinks among the multitudes there. We were apprehensive lest something go wrong at the last minute which would prevent us from honoring our promise. Using the services of an organization which provides this service annually seemed a sure way of having our grape juice reach its intended beneficiaries.

But a very strange thing happened. We traveled to Bnei Brak, delivered the grape juice ourselves to a drop-off spot from where the charity organization had it brought to a warehouse. There it was to remain until it would be transported to Meron in the week prior to Lag BaOmer. However, each time that the organization sent a delivery to Meron that week, our fifteen cases of juice were mistakenly left behind.

This happened despite the fact that this organization is known to be highly reliable, and that my friend and I called their office a number of times that week to ensure that our goods would be on the next truck to Meron. Each time, there was a reason why the cases had been forgotten: the driver had misunderstood the instructions . . . ; he had been unable to locate our cases . . . It was very strange indeed.

On Lag BaOmer morning, our cases were still sitting in the storeroom in Bnei Brak. We were left with no choice but to go to Bnei Brak and transport the cases ourselves. But we wanted to travel to Meron with our friends so that we would be able to celebrate together with them. We also needed their help in carrying the cases of grape juice up Meron's steep hills. So my friend and I made plans to transport the cases by bus to Ashdod in time to catch our chartered bus to Meron.

But we missed the bus.

The bus pulled into the Bnei Brak station at 12:05, five minutes ahead of schedule. My friend, who is known to be punctual, arrived at the bus stop less than one minute after the bus pulled away. It was then that it became clear to me that, for some unknown reason, Heaven was placing obstacles in our path which seemed to be preventing us from accomplishing this mission.

My friend and I were contemplating taking a *sheirut* (group taxi) from Bnei Brak to Meron when suddenly a *sheirut* pulled up in front of us and the driver called out, "Ashdod, Ashdod!"

What good fortune! That time of day, one does not expect to find a *sheirut* to Ashdod. Moreover, the driver, a secular fellow who was quite amiable, hopped out and helped us load our precious cargo onto the van. "Since when does a *sheirut* go to Ashdod this time of day?" we asked the man. "I myself don't know," the driver replied. "It just worked out that way."

A Telling Conversation

As we headed toward Ashdod, we discussed the cost of the trip. Rafi, the driver, wanted a hefty surcharge for transporting the grape juice and we felt that he was asking for too much. I told Rafi that we were on a *mitzvah* mission, and proceeded to relate the entire story to him.

The driver was obviously shaken by my words. Gripping the steering wheel tightly, Rafi told us with emotion that his sister was already married for twelve years without children. "I'm transporting your cases for free," he now declared, "but I want you to do this for my sister: When you go up to Meron, mention my sister and brother-in-law's names and promise the 53 liters of wine for them if they have a baby. I'll worry about bringing the wine next year, *b'ezrat Hashem* (with God's help)."

We arrived in Ashdod on time and Rafi helped us load our cargo onto the chartered bus. "We will stay in touch," he told us happily as we parted.

After Lag BaOmer, I phoned Rafi to say that we had prayed at R' Shimon's tomb on behalf of his sister. He told me that his family had prayed as well.

We did not stay in touch after that conversation.

◈ The Next Encounter

On 15 Tammuz, 5758 (July 9, 1998), we hired a van to take us from Ashdod to Bnei Brak to attend a *bris.* The van had only gone a few blocks when the battery died. The driver could not believe it, as the van was brandnew.

We quickly made our way to a nearby taxi stand and were relieved to find an available van. As we headed on our way, our new driver exclaimed that that very morning at 3 A.M., his sister had given birth to a girl, her first child after thirteen years of marriage.

Upon hearing this, it dawned upon me that the driver had been looking at me strangely soon after I had entered the van. Could it be . . . ?

As I was sitting there wondering, the driver suddenly turned around to me and with a shy smile asked, "Is it possible that you once rode with me?" It was Rafi.

Rafi began to cry and I cried with him. "This morning," he said, "when they woke me up to tell me the news, I said to myself, 'How will I ever find my friends and benefactors to tell them that their prayers had been answered?' That this has happened today can only be from Hashem, so that I could tell you the news."

I was speechless. All I could do at that point was to begin reciting *Tefillas HaDerech* (Prayer for a Journey). Rafi withdrew a *kippah* and placed it on his head. "I have to do this," he explained, "I am coming closer to Judaism. I am *mitchazek* (being strengthened)."

When, with God's help, we will visit Meron this coming Lag BaOmer, we will be joined by a very happy family who is drawing closer to Hashem and His Torah through the wonders which they have merited. And we will be reminded of the incredible workings of *hashgachah pratis* (precise Divine intervention) that brought us to celebrate with them.

His Greatness Revealed

The following was related by R' Yechezkel of Shiniv,[1] who heard it from a God-fearing Jew in Safed when he visited the Holy Land in 1869:

For years, R' Elazar Azkari,[2] author of *Sefer Charedim,* served as a *shamash* (synagogue attendant) in Safed and people assumed him to be an average Jew. Then, on one Lag BaOmer, he visited Meron and was present as the holy kabbalist R' Yitzchak Luria (the *Arizal*) and his disciples celebrated the *hilula* of R' Shimon bar Yochai.

The *Arizal* and his disciples danced with fervor for a very long time. Also present was an elderly man of regal bearing, clothed in white, whose countenance radiated holiness and purity. Some of the time this man danced with the others, while part of the time he danced alone. At one point, he joined hands with R' Elazar Azkari.

During one dance, the *Arizal* suddenly took hold of the old man's hands and danced with him inside the circle for a long time. Then, the *Arizal* took R' Elazar Azkari by the hand and danced with him for a long time with great fervor and joy. Later, when the *Arizal's* disciples expressed wonderment over this, the *Arizal* smiled and said: "If the holy *Tanna* R' Shimon bar Yochai

1. It was related in R' Yechezkel's name by R' Chaim Elazar Shapiro of Munkacz, author of *Minchas Elazar.*

2. 1533-1600.

chose to dance with R' Elazar alone, then could it be beneath the dignity of someone as insignificant as myself to dance with him?" Only then did the disciples begin to realize R' Elazar's true worth, and only then did they discover that they had been joined by the one whose *hilula* they had come to celebrate, R' Shimon bar Yochai *(Masos Yerushalayim).*

More Precious than Gold

⁂ Once, a *chassid* of the *Tzemach Tzaddik* of Viznitza journeyed from Europe to be at Meron on Lag BaOmer. He was unprepared for something that is a rarity in the Land of Israel — a downpour in the spring! When the day of prayer and celebration ended, the *chassid* skidded as he made his way down the muddy mountain. His suit was caked with mud. Anxious that he not miss the boat for the return trip home, he changed into his Sabbath finery, threw his muddied suit into a bag and hurried on his way.

Soon after his return home, he went to visit the *Tzemach Tzaddik* and report on his journey. After greeting his *chassid,* the *Rebbe* asked in jest, "Did you bring me a gift from the Holy Land?" The *chassid* then began to relate his experiences. He told of his mishap in the mud, and mentioned that he had not yet had time to clean his clothing. The *Tzemach Tzaddik* said, "I would greatly appreciate it if you could bring me that garment."

Later, the *Tzemach Tzaddik* held the garment in one hand and with his other hand carefully scraped off some of the dried mud into a clean handkerchief. "I assure you," he told the *chassid,* "that you could not have brought me a more precious gift than this, the holy soil of Meron."

No Cause for Concern

⁂ In the year 1919, Arabs in Palestine made it known that they would attempt to block Jews from making their yearly pilgrimage to Meron in honor of Lag BaOmer.

Living in Safed at that time was the legendary Sefardic kabbalist, R' Shlomo Eliezer ("*Maharsha*") Alfandri, known as "the *Saba Kadisha*" ("The Holy Elder"), who was then past ninety. *Maharsha* Alfandri, who had served as chief rabbi in Istanbul and then Damascus, was revered by Jews the world over as a pure and holy *tzaddik*. Upon learning of the Arab threat, *Maharsha* closeted himself in a room for a night and a day; not even those closest to him were permitted entrance. Finally, he emerged from his seclusion and declared that Jews should travel to Meron as always in advent of Lag BaOmer — and he gave his personal assurance that no harm would befall anyone.

Lag BaOmer passed without incident.

The Forgotten Promise

In *V'Nichtav BaSefer*, R' Yaakov Meir Shechter relates the following:

In the Old City complex of *Battei Machseh*, where R' Shechter lived as a boy, lived an outstanding Sefardic scholar named *Chacham* Shaul Sharbani. *Chacham* Shaul once related that when he was a young man, he and a friend received notices from the ruling Turkish government that they had been drafted to serve in the Turkish Army. It was well known that for a religious Jew to serve in the Turkish Army meant being exposed to serious physical and spiritual dangers. Thus, anyone who received the dreaded notice did everything in his power to free himself from service.

Shaul and his friend devised a plan which stood a fair chance of accomplishing this goal. They both vowed that if God would help them succeed, then they would express their gratitude by traveling to Meron to pray at the tomb of R' Shimon bar Yochai.

The plan worked and they were both exempted from army duty. Shaul Sharbani wasted no time in fulfilling his promise, which involved a week-long journey by donkey or camel. He arrived safely in Meron and poured out his heart in prayer of thanksgiving.

His friend, however, did not join him. For whatever reason, he never made the trip to Meron.

Unfortunately, the friend later received a second draft notice. *Chacham* Shaul was never again asked to serve.

In recounting this episode, R' Schechter writes:

> Both when praying in times of distress and when expressing thanksgiving to God for one's successes, a person must always remember that all his efforts and successes are only through the kindness of God who had mercy upon him and rescued him. Only then can one's successes endure.

R' Isser'l's Reward

Lag BaOmer is the yahrtzeit of R' Moshe Isserles, the famed Rama of Cracow (see "Laws and Customs" in this volume).

In sixteenth-century Cracow lived a Jew named Yisrael Isser, known as "R' Isser'l." R' Isser'l was a noted Torah scholar, philanthropist, and respected communal leader. He manufactured and sold fine silk; among his customers were many of Poland's nobility.

Late one Friday morning, a nobleman entered R' Isser'l's store with the intention of making a huge purchase. Slowly, the nobleman made his way from shelf to shelf, carefully selecting some of R' Isser'l's most expensive merchandise. When noon arrived, the nobleman had completed his selections, but the fabrics still had to be measured before payment could be made. R' Isser'l told his customer:

"Please forgive me, but I must close the store now. It is my practice never to work past noon on Friday, so that I can properly ready myself for the Sabbath. I will measure your merchandise Sunday morning as soon as the store opens and will have it delivered to your door."

His words incensed the nobleman. This purchase would net R' Isser'l a handsome profit. The nobleman wanted the silk *now.* Couldn't R' Isser'l spare the half-hour it would take to measure all the silk? In any case, if the purchase could not be completed now, the nobleman would take his business elsewhere.

R' Isser'l again offered his apologies. He emphasized, "In all my years in business, I never once deviated from my practice of not engaging in business on Friday afternoon."

The nobleman left in a huff. The deal was off.

R' Isser'l's sacrifice was noted in Heaven. It was later revealed to him that as a reward, he would be granted a son who would illuminate the world with his Torah wisdom. R' Isser'l's wife gave birth to a son whom they named Moshe. He grew to become the famed *Rama* of Cracow. רמ״א, *Rama,* is an acronym for ר׳ משה איסר׳לס, *R' Moshe Isserles [son of Isser].*

Lag BaOmer Songs

⸎ אָמַר רַבִּי עֲקִיבָא / Amar Rabbi Akiva ⸎

This popular Lag BaOmer song is from the concluding *mishnah* of Tractate *Yoma*. Its significance is discussed on p. 41.

אָמַר רַבִּי עֲקִיבָא, אַשְׁרֵיכֶם יִשְׂרָאֵל!
לִפְנֵי מִי אַתֶּם מִטַּהֲרִים
וּמִי מְטַהֵר אֶתְכֶם?
אֲבִיכֶם שֶׁבַּשָּׁמַיִם!
וְאוֹמֵר מִקְוֵה יִשְׂרָאֵל ה׳,
מַה מִּקְוֶה מְטַהֵר אֶת הַטְּמֵאִים,
אַף הַקָּדוֹשׁ בָּרוּךְ הוּא מְטַהֵר אֶת יִשְׂרָאֵל.

Rabbi Akiva said: Fortunate are you, O Israel!
Before Whom do you cleanse yourselves?
Who cleanses you?
Your Father in Heaven![1]
And it [also] says: "The mikveh of Israel is Hashem."[2]
Just as a mikveh purifies the contaminated,
so does the Holy One, Blessed is He, purify Israel.

1.The mishnah includes the following phrase which is not in the song: "*As it is stated* (*Ezekiel* 36:25): '*I will sprinkle pure water upon you, and you shall be cleansed.*'"

2. *Jeremiah* 17:13.

◆ בַּר יוֹחָאי / Bar Yochai

◆ This song is sung in communities throughout the world on Lag BaOmer. In the land of Israel, *Sefardim* and many *Ashkenazim* who pray in *Nusach Sefard* also sing it on the Friday night preceding Lag BaOmer at the conclusion of *Kabbalas Shabbos.* In this way, the song is an introduction of sorts to "*Kegavna,*" a teaching from *Zohar* taught by R' Shimon bar Yochai.

Some communites sing "*Bar Yochai*" every Friday night of the year. The initial letters of the song's refrain [בַּר יוֹחָאי נִמְשַׁחְתָּ אַשְׁרֶיךָ שֶׁמֶן שָׂשׂוֹן מֵחֲבֵרֶיךָ] have the same *gematria* (numerical value) as שַׁבַּתָּא (Sabbath in Aramaic, the language of *Zohar* — 703). In R' Shimon bar Yochai's merit, one can achieve a greater spiritual uplift through the *neshamah yeseirah* (additional soul) which every Jew attains as the Sabbath is ushered in (*Tapuchei Zahav*).[1]

The Song's Author

◆ *Bar Yochai* was authored by the kabbalist R' Shimon Labia,[2] who died in the year 1584 when, it is related, he was close to one hundred years old.

As a child, R' Shimon was forced to leave the country of his birth when all the Jews were expelled from Spain in 5252/1492. Eventually, he settled in Fez, Morocco, where he grew up and spent the major part of his life. In the year 5309/1549, R'

1. As mentioned above (p. 70), the *gematria* of שִׁמְעוֹן בַּר יוֹחַאי equals 703, and that of שַׁבָּת is 702, which is considered a *gematria* equivalency (see below, footnote on p. 159).

Some have the custom to sing *Bar Yochai* whenever they visit R' Shimon's tomb in Meron. R' Yoel Teitelbaum, the late Satmar *Rav,* instructed that it be sung when he visited the tomb.

Some sing *Bar Yochai* on the nights of Shavuos and *Hoshanah Rabbah.* Some students of Kabbalah would sing it at the end of every study session of *Sefer HaZohar* (*Tikkunei Shabbos*). *Bar Yochai* is published in the standard edition of *Zohar.*

2. The initial letters of the song's stanzas spell his name.

Shimon left Morocco with the intention of settling in the Holy Land.

On his journey to Eretz Yisrael, R' Shimon stopped off in Tripoli and observed the degenerated state of Torah knowledge and the lax religious observance of the Torah populace. Considering the situation carefully, he decided to give up his cherished dream of living in Eretz Yisrael, and chose rather to remain with the spiritually unfortunate Jews of Libya, to return them to the right path. He succeeded in attaining this objective, but never was able to reach his original destination.

R' Shimon authored an extensive commentary on the *Zohar,* which he did not live to complete or even decide upon a title. Some two hundred years after his death, as his commentary to *Genesis* was being prepared for publication, the famed *Chida* instructed that it be entitled כֶּתֶם פָּז (*Finest Gold*[1]), which has the same *gematria* (numerical equivalency) as שִׁמְעוֹן בֶּן לַבִּיָא ז"ל.[2]

---

1. From *Song of Songs* 5:11. פָּז is also an acronym for פֵּירוּשׁ זֹהַר, *commentary to Zohar* (*Hilula D'Rashbi* citing earlier sources).

R' Asher Zelig Margulies writes that after R' Shimon Labia's death, his gravesite was known as a place of prayer and great salvation. For generations, Jews would flock to his grave and pray that in his merit their entreaties be answered. This did not go unnoticed by the local Arab populace. When Italy invaded Libya and gained control of Tripoli, the Arab community lodged a complaint with the ruling government, contending that the Jews had robbed them of their holy site! Of course, this charge was hotly contested by the leaders of the local Jewish community.

The government decided that there was no recourse but to exhume the grave and attempt to determine who was telling the truth. In the presence of government officials the grave was exhumed. They were shocked beyond words when R' Shimon Labia's body was unearthed — wrapped in a *tallis,* fresh and fully composed as on the day of his death.

2. כֶּתֶם פָּז equals 547, while שִׁמְעוֹן בֶּן לַבִּיָא ז"ל equals 546. In the discipline of *gematria,* two sides of an equation are considered equal even when there is a difference of one. *Bnei Yissoschor* cites two Scriptural proofs of this principle:

The first proof is from *Deuteronomy* 4:25 where the Torah speaks of the Jewish people becoming corrupt after remaining long (וְנוֹשַׁנְתֶּם) in its Land and turning to idol worship. The next verse states that in retribution for this, *you shall soon utterly perish* . . . The Talmud states (*Sanhedrin* 38a) that God was compassionate in sending the Jews into exile 850 years after they entered the Land of Israel, for had they been in the Land for 852 years — the *gematria* of וְנוֹשַׁנְתֶּם — the prophesied curse of *you shall soon utterly perish* . . . would have been fulfilled in all its harshness. It is apparent from this statement that were the Jews to have been exiled after

A Song of Spiritual Ecstasy

In *Hilula D'Rashbi,* R' Asher Zelig Margulies describes the ecstasy with which *"Bar Yochai"* is sung on Lag BaOmer at Meron:

> One cannot describe the tremendous joy, exhilaration and *dveikus* (spiritual attachment) that is felt when the singing of this sacred song begins. One feels all the Heavenly gates opening from the gladness of holiness — more than with any of the other songs that are sung there. The *Sefardim* still sing *"Bar Yochai"* to the very same tune sung by its holy author, while the *Ashkenazim* sing it with slightly different nuances.
>
> Regarding the song's content: It is far more than a play on words as is the way of poetry. Every stanza, word and letter is significant and is based on Scriptural verses, teachings of our Sages, passages from the *Zohar* and the secrets of Kabbalah — concepts which "stand at the pinnacle of the universe."[1] . . . It is no wonder, then, that those who sing it experience such great spiritual upliftment.

The translation and commentary below, from the ArtScroll *Zemiroth* by Rabbi Nosson Scherman, is based on the commentary of R' Asher Zelig Margulies in his *Shir Bar Yochai.*

---

851 years, *one* less than the value of וְנוֹשַׁנְתֶּם, they would have still been liable to incur the full punishment of that verse.

The second proof is where Jacob told Joseph: אֶפְרַיִם וּמְנַשֶּׁה כִּרְאוּבֵן וְשִׁמְעוֹן יִהְיוּ לִי, *Ephraim and Manasseh shall be to me like Reuben and Simeon (Genesis* 48:5). The plain meaning is that Joseph's two sons would have the status of tribes and be considered equal to Reuben and Simeon (the oldest of Jacob's sons). *Ba'al HaTurim* notes that this status is alluded to in the numerical equivalencies of אֶפְרַיִם וּמְנַשֶּׁה to רְאוּבֵן וְשִׁמְעוֹן. In fact, the *gematria* of אֶפְרַיִם וּמְנַשֶּׁה is 732, while that of רְאוּבֵן וְשִׁמְעוֹן is 731.

1. *Berachos* 6b.

בַּר יוֹחָאי נִמְשַׁחְתָּ אַשְׁרֶיךָ,
שֶׁמֶן שָׂשׂוֹן מֵחֲבֵרֶיךָ.

Bar Yochai! You were anointed —
you are fortunate —
With oil of joy from your fellows.

בַּר יוֹחָאי – שֶׁמֶן מִשְׁחַת קֹדֶשׁ,
נִמְשַׁחְתָּ מִמִּדַּת הַקֹּדֶשׁ,
נָשָׂאתָ צִיץ נֵזֶר הַקֹּדֶשׁ,
חָבוּשׁ עַל רֹאשְׁךָ פְּאֵרֶךָ.

בַּר יוֹחָאי נִמְשַׁחְתָּ אַשְׁרֶיךָ, שֶׁמֶן שָׂשׂוֹן מֵחֲבֵרֶיךָ.

Bar Yochai! *With oil of sacred anointment*
you were anointed from the holy measure
You bore the headplate, a crown of holiness,
bound upon your head is your glory.
Bar Yochai! You were anointed — you are fortunate —
With oil of joy from your fellows.

נִמְשַׁחְתָּ – *You were anointed.* Anointment alludes to prophetic knowledge. While R' Shimon bar Yochai was not a prophet, he was granted an unprecedented degree of mystical knowledge, just as a prophet is given his prophecy directly by God.

שֶׁמֶן שָׂשׂוֹן – *With oil of joy.* Prophecy rests only in the midst of joy, but never upon one who is depressed or mournful.

מֵחֲבֵרֶיךָ – *From your fellows.* R' Shimon merited his greatest revelations because he sought to see the good side of his fellow Jews (*Shabbos* 33a) and to defend them against criticism (*Succah* 45b). Thus, his prophetic insights came, in a sense, *from his fellows.*

שֶׁמֶן מִשְׁחַת קֹדֶשׁ – *With oil of sacred anointment.* This first stanza alludes to the *Sefirah* of מַלְכוּת, *kingship.* A king is consecrated to his throne with anointment. The oil which is soft and smooth represents blessing, for the duty of a king is to serve as a conduit of blessing for the nation which depends on him.

נָשָׂאתָ צִיץ נֵזֶר הַקֹּדֶשׁ – *You bore the headplate, a crown of holiness.* Aside from the obvious allusion to kingship, there is a further implication of בִּינָה, *understanding,* which emanates from the mind. Thus, the crown is designated as a *headplate,* for the proper role of the spiritual king is to influence people to repent by bringing them to a

בַּר יוֹחָאי – מוֹשַׁב טוֹב יָשַׁבְתָּ,
יוֹם נַסְתָּ יוֹם אֲשֶׁר בָּרַחְתָּ,
בִּמְעָרַת צוּרִים שֶׁעָמַדְתָּ,
שָׁם קָנִיתָ הוֹדְךָ וַהֲדָרֶךָ.
בַּר יוֹחָאי נִמְשַׁחְתָּ אַשְׁרֶיךָ, שֶׁמֶן שָׂשׂוֹן מֵחֲבֵרֶיךָ.

Bar Yochai! *In a goodly dwelling did you settle*
on the day you ran, the day you fled,
In rocky caves where you stopped —
there you acquired your glory and your strength.
Bar Yochai! You were anointed — you are fortunate —
With oil of joy from your fellows.

בַּר יוֹחָאי – עֲצֵי שִׁטִּים עוֹמְדִים,
לִמּוּדֵי יהוה הֵם לוֹמְדִים,
אוֹר מֻפְלָא אוֹר הַיְקוֹד הֵם יוֹקְדִים,

---

proper understanding of their mission on earth.

מוֹשַׁב טוֹב יָשַׁבְתָּ — *In a goodly dwelling did you settle.* R' Shimon was condemned to execution by the Romans because he criticized them as selfish. All their striving to improve the land by building roads, markets, bridges and bathhouses was for their perverse pleasures. With his son Elazar, he fled to a cave in the Galil where he remained for thirteen years. There, God miraculously provided them with a carob tree and a spring for their food and water. As a result of his years of total concentration on Torah study in this Heavenly provided *goodly dwelling,* he was able to rise to his later height.

יוֹם נַסְתָּ יוֹם אֲשֶׁר בָּרַחְתָּ — *On the day you ran, the day you fled.* The apparent redundancy has a purpose. R' Shimon is likened to Moses, for just as Moses was God's agent to present Israel with the revealed Torah, so R' Shimon was His agent to present the mystical Torah; Moses and R' Shimon, because they had parallel missions, are like one person. Each was forced to flee from a pursuing government: Moses from Pharaoh and R' Shimon from Rome. And each was endangered because an informant went to authorities. Therefore the doubled expression — God's lawgiver had to flee twice.

עֲצֵי שִׁטִּים עוֹמְדִים — *Like standing shittim beams.* The Torah describes the walls of the Tabernacle as being made of *standing shittim beams.* Those who study the *teachings of God* are referred to as the sturdy beams who uphold the sacred dwelling of God.

הֲלֹא הֵמָּה יוֹרוּךָ מוֹרֶיךָ.

בַּר יוֹחָאי נִמְשַׁחְתָּ אַשְׁרֶיךָ, שֶׁמֶן שָׂשׂוֹן מֵחֲבֵרֶיךָ.

Bar Yochai! *Like standing shittim beams,*
the teachings of God they study
An extraordinary light is the light of the fire that they kindle
— they, your teachers, will teach you.
Bar Yochai! You were anointed — you are fortunate —
With oil of joy from your fellows.

בַּר יוֹחָאי – וְלִשְׂדֵה תַּפּוּחִים,
עָלִיתָ לִלְקוֹט בּוֹ מֶרְקָחִים,
סוֹד תּוֹרָה בְּצִיצִים וּפְרָחִים,
נַעֲשֶׂה אָדָם נֶאֱמַר בַּעֲבוּרֶךָ.

בַּר יוֹחָאי נִמְשַׁחְתָּ אַשְׁרֶיךָ, שֶׁמֶן שָׂשׂוֹן מֵחֲבֵרֶיךָ.

Bar Yochai! *You came to a Field of Apples*
and entered it to pick confections:
The mystery of Torah with blossoms and flowers —
"Let us create man" was said because of you.
Bar Yochai! You were anointed — you are fortunate —
With oil of joy from your fellows.

וְלִשְׂדֵה תַּפּוּחִים — *To a Field of Apples.* In kabbalistic terminology, the *Field of Apples* refers to a degree of holiness as exalted as that of the Garden of Eden before Adam's sin.

מֶרְקָחִים — *Confections.* The term refers to a mixture of spices or of foods to create a sum which is finer than any of the parts. R' Shimon's teachings are praised as a blend of all the elements of Torah knowledge presented in a manner best calculated to bring out their maximum wisdom and beauty.

סוֹד תּוֹרָה בְּצִיצִים וּפְרָחִים — *The mystery of Torah with blossoms and flowers.* The praise of his all-encompassing learning continues. The *blossoms* and *flowers* refer to sidelights to knowledge that offer further enrichment. The mysteries revealed to and taught by R' Shimon were given extra beauty and dimension by him.

נַעֲשֶׂה אָדָם נֶאֱמַר בַּעֲבוּרֶךָ — *"Let us create man," was said because of you.* R' Shimon's greatness was such that the creation of man was justified for his sake alone.

בַּר יוֹחָאי – נֶאֱזַרְתָּ בִּגְבוּרָה,
וּבְמִלְחֶמֶת אֵשׁ דַּת הַשַּׁעְרָה,
וְחֶרֶב הוֹצֵאתָ מִתַּעְרָהּ,
שָׁלַפְתָּ נֶגֶד צוֹרְרֶיךָ.

בַּר יוֹחָאי נִמְשַׁחְתָּ אַשְׁרֶיךָ, שֶׁמֶן שָׂשׂוֹן מֵחֲבֵרֶיךָ.

Bar Yochai! *You were girded with strength,*
and in the war of the fiery Torah up to the gate
You pulled a sword from its scabbard,
you drew it against your enemies.

Bar Yochai! You were anointed — you are fortunate —
With oil of joy from your fellows.

בַּר יוֹחָאי – לִמְקוֹם אַבְנֵי שַׁיִשׁ,
הִגַּעְתָּ וּפְנֵי אַרְיֵה לַיִשׁ,

נֶאֱזַרְתָּ בִּגְבוּרָה – *You were girded with strength.* R' Shimon had the strength to defy the Romans and speak out against them.

וּבְמִלְחֶמֶת אֵשׁ דַּת הַשַּׁעְרָה – *And in the war of the fiery Torah up to the gate.* The שַׁעַר הָעִיר, *gate of the city,* is an expression frequently used in Scripture to denote the meeting place of the sages or the court. It was in the gatherings of the greatest scholars that R' Shimon distinguished himself as an outstanding warrior in the battle for Torah.

חֶרֶב – *Sword.* The efforts of a *tzaddik* to help his people against those who would harm them are referred to as the *sword* he employs in their behalf.

צוֹרְרֶיךָ – *Your enemies.* The prosecuting angels who seek to condemn Israel were regarded by R' Shimon as *his* enemies. He fought them by engaging in the struggle for Torah; he sought to teach the people Torah in greater depth so that they could rise to greater spiritual levels.

לִמְקוֹם אַבְנֵי שַׁיִשׁ הִגַּעְתָּ – *To a place of marble stones, you arrived.* The reference is to *Chagigah* 14b, where R' Akiva, the teacher of R' Shimon, speaks of the sparkling marble in Paradise. The reference was not understood, for only one who had been there, as R' Akiva had, could conceive of it. To R' Shimon, however, the mystery was revealed.

וּפְנֵי אַרְיֵה לַיִשׁ – *And before a huge lion.* The term "lion" is used to describe a great and exalted soul. The unknown one was revealed to R' Shimon. The secret of the *marble* was the soul of some very great personage who had gone to his rest.

גַּם גֻּלַּת כּוֹתֶרֶת עַל עַיִשׁ,
תְּשׁוּרִי וּמִי יְשׁוּרֶךָ.
בַּר יוֹחָאי נִמְשַׁחְתָּ אַשְׁרֶיךָ, שֶׁמֶן שָׂשׂוֹן מֵחֲבֵרֶיךָ.

Bar Yochai! *To a place of marble stones,*
you arrived, and before a huge lion.
Even a rounded crown upon a constellation's star
you perceived — but none can perceive you.
Bar Yochai! You were anointed — you are fortunate —
With oil of joy from your fellows.

בַּר יוֹחָאי — בְּקֹדֶשׁ הַקֳּדָשִׁים,
קַו יָרֹק מְחַדֵּשׁ חֳדָשִׁים,
שֶׁבַע שַׁבָּתוֹת סוֹד חֲמִשִּׁים,
קָשַׁרְתָּ קִשְׁרֵי שִׁי״ן קְשָׁרֶיךָ.
בַּר יוֹחָאי נִמְשַׁחְתָּ אַשְׁרֶיךָ, שֶׁמֶן שָׂשׂוֹן מֵחֲבֵרֶיךָ.

גֻּלַּת כּוֹתֶרֶת — *A rounded crown.* Because R' Shimon was zealous in his desire to help his fellow Jews whenever he could, he symbolizes the attribute of חֶסֶד, *kindness,* an attribute that is the source of many others. Thus it is like a *crown.*

עַיִשׁ — *A constellation's star.* The *Midrash* says that God stopped the floodwaters in Noah's time by sealing the heavens with two stars. Thus, the stars were used to do an act of kindness to mankind.

בְּקֹדֶשׁ הַקֳּדָשִׁים — *In the Holy of Holies.* A person's בִּינָה, *understanding,* is his personal *Holy of Holies,* for without it, his inspirational flashes of wisdom come to naught or they can be developed grotesquely.

קַו יָרֹק — *A green line.* The development of wisdom through understanding and application is called a *line:* the flash of חָכְמָה, *wisdom,* is likened to a "point" until it is utilized and developed. As it spreads out into development and application, it is likened to a spreading line.

יָרֹק — *Green.* Developing wisdom is symbolized by green, the color of growing, life-supporting vegetation.

שֶׁבַע שַׁבָּתוֹת סוֹד חֲמִישִּׁים — *Seven weeks are the secret of the fifty. Seven weeks* represent forty-nine levels of understanding. The loftiest level of understanding is the fiftieth. Thus the stages of development are described as forty-nine, leading up to the fiftieth. So too, there were forty-nine days of preparation from the Exodus up to the fiftieth day when the Ten Commandments were given.

קִשְׁרֵי שִׁי״ן — *The bonds of Shin.* That the

Bar Yochai! In the Holy of Holies,
a green line creates new manifestations
Seven weeks are the secret of the fifty,
you bound the bonds of Shin as your bonds.
Bar Yochai! You were anointed — you are fortunate —
With oil of joy from your fellows.

בַּר יוֹחָאי – **יוּ״ד** חָכְמָה קְדוּמָה,
הִשְׁקַפְתָּ לִכְבוּדָּה פְּנִימָה,
ל״ב נְתִיבוֹת רֵאשִׁית תְּרוּמָה,
אַתְּ כְּרוּב מִמְשַׁח זִיו אוֹרֶךְ.
בַּר יוֹחָאי נִמְשַׁחְתָּ אַשְׁרֶיךָ, שֶׁמֶן שָׂשׂוֹן מֵחֲבֵרֶיךָ.

Bar Yochai! *The Yud of earliest wisdom,*
you gazed into its innermost honor,
The thirty-two paths of the very first tithe,
you are like a cherub anointed with the glow
of your illumination.
Bar Yochai! You were anointed — you are fortunate —
With oil of joy from your fellows.

---

letter *Shin* must be engraved upon *tefillin* is a law transmitted orally to Moses at Sinai. Knowledge of the reasons for this law represents the highest level of human wisdom — the knowledge of God's will. The *tefillin* are bound upon the heads of Jews and, as the Sages explain, the nations will fear Israel when they perceive that God's will, as it were, is bound around the heads of Jews.

יוּ״ד חָכְמָה קְדוּמָה — *The Yud of earliest wisdom.* The letter י, *Yud,* because it is tiny, like a point, represents the first spark of wisdom. All knowledge begins with an idea — a "spark" or a "point" — which must then be broadened, deepened, and applied. It is the *earliest* of all emanations because it is the closest to God's Own wisdom.

הִשְׁקַפְתָּ לִכְבוּדָּה פְּנִימָה — *You gazed into its innermost honor.* R' Shimon perceived the innermost secrets of honor. Wisdom is referred to as honor.

ל״ב נְתִיבוֹת — *The thirty-two paths.* There are thirty-two methods of exegetical understanding.

רֵאשִׁית תְּרוּמָה — *Of the very first tithe.* Torah is referred to as both רֵאשִׁית, *first,* to indicate its paramount importance, and תְּרוּמָה, *tithe,* according to kabbalis-

בַּר יוֹחָאי – אוֹר מֻפְלָא רוּם מַעְלָה,
יָרֵאתָ מִלְּהַבִּיט כִּי רַב לָהּ,
תַּעֲלוּמָה וְאַיִן קוֹרֵא לָהּ,
נַמְתָּ עַיִן לֹא תְשׁוּרֶךָּ.

בַּר יוֹחָאי נִמְשַׁחְתָּ אַשְׁרֶיךָ, שֶׁמֶן שָׂשׂוֹן מֵחֲבֵרֶיךָ.

Bar Yochai! *At a wondrous light in lofty heights*
you feared to stare for it is great.
Such hiddenness that one calls her, "Naught".
You declared that no eye could glimpse You.

Bar Yochai! You were anointed — you are fortunate —
With oil of joy from your fellows.

בַּר יוֹחָאי – אַשְׁרֵי יוֹלַדְתֶּךָ,
אַשְׁרֵי הָעָם הֵם לוֹמְדֶיךָ,
וְאַשְׁרֵי הָעוֹמְדִים עַל סוֹדֶךָ,
לְבוּשֵׁי חֹשֶׁן תֻּמֶּיךָ וְאוּרֶיךָ.

בַּר יוֹחָאי נִמְשַׁחְתָּ אַשְׁרֶיךָ, שֶׁמֶן שָׂשׂוֹן מֵחֲבֵרֶיךָ.

Bar Yochai! *Fortunate is she who bore you,*
fortunate is the people that learns from you.
And fortunate are those who can plumb your mystery,
garbed in the priestly breastplate
and Your Ineffable Name.

Bar Yochai! You were anointed — you are fortunate —
With oil of joy from your fellows.

---

tic literature. Specifically R' Shimon referred to his own Torah knowledge as תְּרוּמָה, lit., *separation,* because he separated it from the teachings of his mentor R' Akiva.

אוֹר מֻפְלָא — *[At] a wondrous light.* The reference is to perceptions of God that are too holy, even for human beings of R' Shimon's stature. God's *Crown* is too far removed from human intelligence for him to glimpse.

יָרֵאתָ מִלְּהַבִּיט — *You feared to stare.* The greater one is, the more conscious he is of what is beyond him.

◆§ וַאֲמַרְתֶּם כֹּה לֶחָי §◆ – Va'amartem Ko Lechoi

◆§ The following popular Lag BaOmer song was composed by *Chacham* Yosef Chaim of Baghdad,[1] one of Sefardic Jewry's most towering personalities in recent centuries. He was a prolific author; his *Ben Ish Chai* is an indispensable halachic work for those of Sefardic origin and is studied by *Ashkenazim* as well, as is his *Ben Yehoyada* on the Aggadic portions of *Talmud Bavli.* He authored many other works spanning the full range of Torah thought.

Chacham Yosef Chaim set aside a special room for seclusion where day and night he studied all aspects of Torah — Talmud, Halachah, Aggadah and Kabbalah. He worked tirelessly at his own spiritual perfection. He fasted all day for six consecutive years, only tasting food at night. A well was dug in his home so that a *mikveh* would be available to him for frequent immersions. Each night at midnight, he would recite *Tikun Chatzos,* the special prayers mourning the Destruction and beseeching Heaven for the Redemption, and he would recite the *Shacharis Shemoneh Esrei* at sunrise, the most opportune time.

The dean of kabbalists of Jerusalem, R' Chaim Shaul Dowek,[2] testified, "All the *Ben Ish Chai's* words were ultimately based on inferences from the writings of the *Arizal,*" and that "the pathways of the heavens were clear to him."

He authored *Hilula Rabba* on Lag BaOmer and was a composer of supplications and songs for many occasions, including *"Va'amartem Ko Lechoi."*

The initial letters of the song's stanzas follow the order of the *Aleph-Beis.* The translation and commentary below is drawn from a wide range of sources.

---

1. 1832-1909.

2. R' Chaim Shaul was the teacher of the noted kabbalist R' Yeshayah Asher Zelig Margulies, whose works are quoted throughout this volume.

וַאֲמַרְתֶּם כֹּה לֶחָי, רַבִּי שִׁמְעוֹן בַּר יוֹחָאי,
וַאֲמַרְתֶּם כֹּה לֶחָי, אֲדוֹנֵינוּ בַּר יוֹחָאי.

And you shall say: "Such [success] for life —
Rabbi Shimon bar Yochai!
And you shall say: "Such [success] for life —
our master, Bar Yochai!

אִישׁ אֱלֹהִים קָדוֹשׁ הוּא, אַשְׁרֵי עַיִן רָאַתְהוּ,
לֵב חָכָם יַשְׂכִּיל פִּיהוּ, אֲדוֹנֵינוּ בַּר יוֹחָאי.

וַאֲמַרְתֶּם כֹּה לֶחָי, רַבִּי שִׁמְעוֹן בַּר יוֹחָאי,
וַאֲמַרְתֶּם כֹּה לֶחָי, אֲדוֹנֵינוּ בַּר יוֹחָאי.

A man of God, holy is he,
praiseworthy is the eye that saw him.
A wise heart will comprehend his words —
our master Bar Yochai! And you shall say . . .

בָּרוּךְ הוּא מִפִּי עֶלְיוֹן, קָדוֹשׁ הוּא מֵהֵרָיוֹן,
מְאוֹר גָּלִיל הָעֶלְיוֹן, אֲדוֹנֵינוּ בַּר יוֹחָאי.

וַאֲמַרְתֶּם כֹּה לֶחָי, רַבִּי שִׁמְעוֹן בַּר יוֹחָאי,
וַאֲמַרְתֶּם כֹּה לֶחָי, אֲדוֹנֵינוּ בַּר יוֹחָאי.

Blessed is he from the mouth of the Supreme One,
sanctified was he from conception,
the light of the Upper Galilee —
our master, Bar Yochai! And you shall say . . .

גִּבּוֹר וְאִישׁ מִלְחָמָה, בְּדַת תּוֹרָה תְמִימָה,
מָלֵא מַדָּע וְחָכְמָה, אֲדוֹנֵינוּ בַּר יוֹחָאי.

וַאֲמַרְתֶּם כֹּה לֶחָי, רַבִּי שִׁמְעוֹן בַּר יוֹחָאי,
וַאֲמַרְתֶּם כֹּה לֶחָי, אֲדוֹנֵינוּ בַּר יוֹחָאי.

וַאֲמַרְתֶּם כֹּה לֶחָי — *Such [success] for life.* I.e., May we enjoy a life of good fortune and blessing in Rabbi Shimon's merit. See commentaries to *I Samuel* 25:6 on which this refrain is based.

Mighty and a man of battle
in the statutes of the perfect Torah,
filled with knowledge and wisdom —
our master, Bar Yochai! And you shall say . . .

דָּרַשׁ כָּל תַּעֲלוּמוֹת, בְּעֹז וְתַעֲצֻמוֹת,
עָלָה מַעֲלוֹת רָמוֹת, אֲדוֹנֵינוּ בַּר יוֹחָאי.

וַאֲמַרְתֶּם כֹּה לֶחָי, רַבִּי שִׁמְעוֹן בַּר יוֹחָאי,
וַאֲמַרְתֶּם כֹּה לֶחָי, אֲדוֹנֵינוּ בַּר יוֹחָאי.

He expounded upon all mysteries
with might and power,
he ascended to exalted levels —
our master, Bar Yochai! And you shall say . . .

הֶחְבָּא בְּתוֹךְ מְעָרָה, מִפְּנֵי הַגְּזֵרָה,
שָׁם לָמַד סִתְרֵי תוֹרָה, אֲדוֹנֵינוּ בַּר יוֹחָאי.

וַאֲמַרְתֶּם כֹּה לֶחָי, רַבִּי שִׁמְעוֹן בַּר יוֹחָאי,
וַאֲמַרְתֶּם כֹּה לֶחָי, אֲדוֹנֵינוּ בַּר יוֹחָאי.

He hid in the cave
because of the decree,
there he learned the Torah's secrets —
our master, Bar Yochai! And you shall say . . .

וְשָׁם נִבְרָא מַעְיָן לוֹ, וְחָרוּב לְמַאֲכָלוֹ,
מַה טּוֹב חֶלְקוֹ וְחֶבְלוֹ, אֲדוֹנֵינוּ בַּר יוֹחָאי.

וַאֲמַרְתֶּם כֹּה לֶחָי, רַבִּי שִׁמְעוֹן בַּר יוֹחָאי,
וַאֲמַרְתֶּם כֹּה לֶחָי, אֲדוֹנֵינוּ בַּר יוֹחָאי.

There, a wellspring was created for him,
and a carob tree for his sustenance,
how good is his portion and his lot —
our master, Bar Yochai! And you shall say . . .

זֵכֶר צַדִּיק לִבְרָכָה, דֵּין רֵיכָא וּבַר רֵיכָא,
זָכָה וְרַבִּים זִכָּה , אֲדוֹנֵינוּ בַּר יוֹחָאי.

וַאֲמַרְתֶּם כֹּה לֶחָי, רַבִּי שִׁמְעוֹן בַּר יוֹחָאי,
וַאֲמַרְתֶּם כֹּה לֶחָי, אֲדוֹנֵינוּ בַּר יוֹחָאי.

The memory of the righteous is for a blessing,
this was a king the son of a king,
he was meritorious and gained merit for the multitudes —
our master, Bar Yochai! *And you shall say . . .*

חִדֵּשׁ כַּמָּה הֲלָכוֹת, הֵן בַּמִּשְׁנָה עֲרוּכוֹת,
זֶה הַמַּרְגִּיז מַמְלָכוֹת, אֲדוֹנֵינוּ בַּר יוֹחָאי.

וַאֲמַרְתֶּם כֹּה לֶחָי, רַבִּי שִׁמְעוֹן בַּר יוֹחָאי,
וַאֲמַרְתֶּם כֹּה לֶחָי, אֲדוֹנֵינוּ בַּר יוֹחָאי.

He originated many laws,
they are arranged in the Mishnah,
this one who shook kingdoms —
our master, Bar Yochai! *And you shall say . . .*

טִהֵר אֶת עִיר טְבֶרְיָה, עָשָׂה אוֹתָהּ נְקִיָּה,

זֵכֶר צַדִּיק לִבְרָכָה— *The memory of the righteous is for a blessing. (Proverbs* 10:7). In his *Hillula Rabba, Chacham* Yosef Chaim writes that the name שִׁמְעוֹן, when spelling out each letter as it is pronounced [שִׁין מֵם עַיִן וָו נוּן], has the same *gematria* as זֵכֶר צַדִּיק לִבְרָכָה (688).

דֵּין רֵיכָא וּבַר רֵיכָא — *This was a king, the son of a king.* This phrase is borrowed from *Bava Basra* 4a. R' Shimon was referred to as *king,* for he perceived the innermost secrets of wisdom. "Who is your king? Rabbi Shimon bar Yochai, master of Torah, master of wisdom" (*Zohar,* Vol. III, 79b).

R' Shimon's father Yochai was a distinguished personage (see *Pesachim* 112a).

זֶה הַמַּרְגִּיז מַמְלָכוֹת — *This one who shook kingdoms.* As related in *Zohar,* when R' Shimon was brought to Meron for burial, a Heavenly voice proclaimed: *This is the man who made the land tremble, who made kingdoms quake!* (from *Isaiah* 14:16).

טִהֵר אֶת עִיר טְבֶרְיָה, עָשָׂה אוֹתָהּ נְקִיָּה — *He purified the city of Tiberias, made it clean.* The *Midrash* relates that upon emerging from the cave in which they had spent thirteen years in hiding, R' Shimon and his son R' Elazar made use

הודו לו מִשְּׁמַיָּא, אֲדוֹנֵינוּ בַּר יוֹחָאי.

וַאֲמַרְתֶּם כֹּה לֶחָי, רַבִּי שִׁמְעוֹן בַּר יוֹחָאי,
וַאֲמַרְתֶּם כֹּה לֶחָי, אֲדוֹנֵינוּ בַּר יוֹחָאי.

He purified the city of Tiberias, and he cleansed it,
they praised him from Heaven —
our master, Bar Yochai! *And you shall say . . .*

יָדַע כָּל הַנִּסְתָּרוֹת, דְּבָרָיו עוֹשִׂים פֵּרוֹת,
בִּטֵּל כַּמָּה גְזֵרוֹת, אֲדוֹנֵינוּ בַּר יוֹחָאי.

וַאֲמַרְתֶּם כֹּה לֶחָי, רַבִּי שִׁמְעוֹן בַּר יוֹחָאי,
וַאֲמַרְתֶּם כֹּה לֶחָי, אֲדוֹנֵינוּ בַּר יוֹחָאי.

He knew all the hidden matters, his words bear fruit,
he annulled many decrees —
our master, Bar Yochai! *And you shall say . . .*

---

of the hot springs of Tiberias to heal the wounds brought about by their years in the abrasive sand. Afterwards, R' Shimon acted upon his son's suggestion that they find some way to benefit the city in appreciation for their having benefited from it.

At that time, *Kohanim* were forced to circumvent the roads of Tiberias because bodies of Jews killed during the Roman onslaught were reportedly buried on these roads at unknown locations. R' Shimon took lupines, cut them and cast them on the Tiberias roads. Miraculously, the bodies buried there rose in the ground, shifting the earth above. The bodies were then transferred to a cemetery and the roads were cleaned of any impurity. (*Bereishis Rabbah* 79:6; see also *Shabbos* 33b-34a and *Yerushalmi Shevi'is* 9:1)).

In *Emunas Itecha,* R' Moshe Wolfson discusses the significance of R' Shimon's purifying the city in which his teacher, R' Akiva, is buried and where the Great *Sanhedrin* (Supreme Court) will first convene at the time of the Redemption (see *Rambam, Hilchos Sanhedrin* 14:12).

בִּטֵּל כַּמָּה גְזֵרוֹת — *He annulled many decrees. Zohar* (Vol. I, 255b) relates that at one point it was revealed to R' Shimon that the world was deserving of destruction. Utilizing his own merit, R' Shimon dispatched an angel to go before the Heavenly Throne and plead for the decree's annulment. His entreaties were accepted and a Heavenly voice proclaimed: "Praiseworthy is your lot, Rabbi Shimon! The Holy One, Blessed is He, decrees Above, and you cause the decree to be annulled below. Regarding you it is said, *He does the will*

כָּל יָמָיו אֲשֶׁר חָיָה, אוֹת הַקֶּשֶׁת לֹא נִהְיָה,
כִּי הוּא אוֹת עוֹלָם הָיָה, אֲדוֹנֵינוּ בַּר יוֹחָאי.

וַאֲמַרְתֶּם כֹּה לֶחָי, רַבִּי שִׁמְעוֹן בַּר יוֹחָאי,
וַאֲמַרְתֶּם כֹּה לֶחָי, אֲדוֹנֵינוּ בַּר יוֹחָאי.

All the days he lived,
the sign of the rainbow did not appear,
for he was a sign of the world —
our master, Bar Yochai! *And you shall say . . .*

לְכָל יִשְׂרָאֵל הֵאִיר, בְּסוֹד תּוֹרָה הַבָּהִיר,
כְּאוֹר הַחַמָּה מַזְהִיר, אֲדוֹנֵינוּ בַּר יוֹחָאי.

וַאֲמַרְתֶּם כֹּה לֶחָי, רַבִּי שִׁמְעוֹן בַּר יוֹחָאי,
וַאֲמַרְתֶּם כֹּה לֶחָי, אֲדוֹנֵינוּ בַּר יוֹחָאי.

To all of Israel he brought light,
through the secret of the glowing Torah,
as brilliant as the light of the sun —
our master, Bar Yochai! *And you shall say . . .*

---

of those who revere Him" (Psalms 145:19). *Zohar* makes other references to R' Shimon's power in this regard.

In *Michtav Me'Eliyahu* (Vol. III, p. 186), R' Eliyahu Dessler explains the concept of צַדִּיק גּוֹזֵר וְהַקָּדוֹשׁ בָּרוּךְ הוּא מְקַיֵּם, *A tzaddik decrees and the Holy One, Blessed is He, fulfills*: "Surely, the intent is *not* that the *tzaddik* can decree something that contravenes the will of God, Heaven forfend. Rather, it is as the Sages teach that there are *tzaddikim* in whose merit the entire world exists . . . and when a *tzaddik* on this exalted level perceives that something is causing the glory of God to be hidden, it is correct that he ask God to withhold it, even if this means altering His way of conducting [the affairs of this world] . . ."

אוֹת הַקֶּשֶׁת לֹא נִהְיָה — *The sign of the rainbow did not appear.* The rainbow is the sign of God's covenant with Noah that never again would all of mankind be destroyed (*Genesis* 9:11-12). As long as Rabbi Shimon bar Yochai lived, the sign of the rainbow was not needed (*Yerushalmi Berachos* 9:1). See following comment.

כִּי הוּא אוֹת עוֹלָם הָיָה — *For he was a sign of the world. Zohar* (Vol. III, 15a) states that the אוֹת, *sign,* of the rainbow was not needed in the generation of R' Shimon, who himself was a *sign* of the world's continuity, for in his merit, God

מָקוֹם בָּחַר בִּשְׁמַיָּא, עִם הַנָּבִיא אֲחִיָּה,
זֶה מִבְּנֵי עֲלִיָּה, אֲדוֹנֵינוּ בַּר יוֹחָאי.

וַאֲמַרְתֶּם כֹּה לֶחָי, רַבִּי שִׁמְעוֹן בַּר יוֹחָאי,
וַאֲמַרְתֶּם כֹּה לֶחָי, אֲדוֹנֵינוּ בַּר יוֹחָאי.

He chose a place in Heaven,
with the prophet Achiyah,
this man of the highest level —
our master, Bar Yochai! *And you shall say . . .*

נֶחְמָד מְאֹד לְמַעֲלָה, זָכָה לִיקָר וּגְדוּלָּה,
כֶּתֶר עֶלְיוֹן לוֹ נִגְלָה, אֲדוֹנֵינוּ בַּר יוֹחָאי.

וַאֲמַרְתֶּם כֹּה לֶחָי, רַבִּי שִׁמְעוֹן בַּר יוֹחָאי,
וַאֲמַרְתֶּם כֹּה לֶחָי, אֲדוֹנֵינוּ בַּר יוֹחָאי.

Exceedingly pleasing was he on High,
he merited honor and distinction,
the Supreme Crown to him was revealed —
our master, Bar Yochai! *And you shall say . . .*

סִינַי סִינַי לוֹ נִקְרָא, אֲרִי שֶׁבַּחֲבוּרָה,

---

would rescind any destructive decree.

עִם הַנָּבִיא אֲחִיָּה — *With the prophet Aciyah*. The prophet Achiyah the Shilonite was the teacher of Elijah the Prophet. *Zohar* states that the soul of Achiyah taught secrets of the Torah to R' Shimon bar Yochai. R' Shimon once declared that he and Achiyah the Shilonite had sufficient merit between them to earn the reward of the World to Come for all generations, from the time of Abraham until the Messiah's arrival (*Bereishis Rabbah* 35:2).

זֶה מִבְּנֵי עֲלִיָּה — *This man of the highest level*. R' Shimon declared that he and his son were בְּנֵי עֲלִיָּה, *people of the highest level,* who receive the countenance of the Divine Presence (*Succah* 45b).

כֶּתֶר עֶלְיוֹן לוֹ נִגְלָה — *The Supreme Crown to him was revealed*. A kabbalistic concept.

סִינַי, סִינַי, לוֹ נִקְרָא — *"Sinai, Sinai," he was called*. A reference to *Zohar,* Vol. III, p. 276b. In *Zohar,* both Moses and R' Shimon bar Yochai, whose soul was a *nitzutz* (spark) of Moses, are often referred to as "Sinai." In *Tikkunei Zohar,* Elijah the Prophet tells R' Shimon, "Holy Lamp, surely your mouth is [the essence of] Sinai" (*Tikun* 22, p. 64a).

אֲרִי שֶׁבַּחֲבוּרָה — *The lion of the group.*

מִמֶּנּוּ תֵּצֵא תּוֹרָה, אֲדוֹנֵינוּ בַּר יוֹחָאי.

וַאֲמַרְתֶּם כֹּה לֶחָי, רַבִּי שִׁמְעוֹן בַּר יוֹחָאי,
וַאֲמַרְתֶּם כֹּה לֶחָי, אֲדוֹנֵינוּ בַּר יוֹחָאי.

"Sinai, Sinai," he was called,
the lion of the group,
from him Torah would go forth —
our master, Bar Yochai! *And you shall say . . .*

עָשָׂה שִׁבְעִים תִּקּוּנִים, יְקָרִים מִפְּנִינִים,
בָּם תִּקֵּן הָעֶלְיוֹנִים, אֲדוֹנֵינוּ בַּר יוֹחָאי.

וַאֲמַרְתֶּם כֹּה לֶחָי, רַבִּי שִׁמְעוֹן בַּר יוֹחָאי,
וַאֲמַרְתֶּם כֹּה לֶחָי, אֲדוֹנֵינוּ בַּר יוֹחָאי.

He made seventy "improvements,"
more precious than pearls,
through them he perfected the Upper Worlds —
our master, Bar Yochai! *And you shall say . . .*

פָּתַח פִּיו בְּחָכְמָה, הוֹצִיא אוֹר תַּעֲלוּמָה,
תִּקֵּן זָהֳרֵי חַמָּה, אֲדוֹנֵינוּ בַּר יוֹחָאי.

וַאֲמַרְתֶּם כֹּה לֶחָי, רַבִּי שִׁמְעוֹן בַּר יוֹחָאי,
וַאֲמַרְתֶּם כֹּה לֶחָי, אֲדוֹנֵינוּ בַּר יוֹחָאי.

He opened his mouth with wisdom,
he brought forth the hidden light,
he perfected the radiance of the sun —
our master, Bar Yochai! *And you shall say . . .*

I.e., the scholar who was greater than his colleagues; from *Shabbos* 111b.

עָשָׂה שִׁבְעִים תִּקּוּנִים — *He effected seventy "improvements."* R' Shimon authored *Tikkunei Zohar* (lit. *Improvements of Radiance*), seventy mystical expositions on the Torah's opening words, בְּרֵאשִׁית בָּרָא אֱלֹהִים.

יְקָרָה מִפְּנִינִם — *More precious than pearls. Proverbs* 3:15.

תִּקֵּן זָהֳרֵי חַמָּה — *He perfected the radiance of the sun.* זָהֳרֵי חַמָּה, *radiance of the sun,* is a metaphor for סֵפֶר הַזֹּהַר, *The Book of Radiance.*

צַדִּיק יְסוֹד הָעוֹלָם, גִּלָּה מִדְרָשׁ הַנֶּעְלָם,
יָכֹל לִפְטֹר הָעוֹלָם, אֲדוֹנֵינוּ בַּר יוֹחָאי.

וַאֲמַרְתֶּם כֹּה לֶחָי, רַבִּי שִׁמְעוֹן בַּר יוֹחָאי,
וַאֲמַרְתֶּם כֹּה לֶחָי, אֲדוֹנֵינוּ בַּר יוֹחָאי.

A righteous one — foundation of the world,
he revealed the "Hidden Midrash,"
he could exonerate the entire world —
our master, Bar Yochai! *And you shall say . . .*

קוֹלוֹ זִמֵּר עָרִיצִים, וְהִכְרִית אֶת הַקּוֹצִים,
וְהִצִּיל אֶת הַלְּחוּצִים, אֲדוֹנֵינוּ בַּר יוֹחָאי.

וַאֲמַרְתֶּם כֹּה לֶחָי, רַבִּי שִׁמְעוֹן בַּר יוֹחָאי,
וַאֲמַרְתֶּם כֹּה לֶחָי, אֲדוֹנֵינוּ בַּר יוֹחָאי.

His voice diminished powerful foes,
he cut away the thorns and rescued the oppressed —
our master, Bar Yochai! *And you shall say . . .*

צַדִּיק יְסוֹד עוֹלָם — *A righteous one, foundation of the world.* This description, from *Proverbs* 10:25, is used in *Zohar* in reference to R' Shimon (Vol. I. p. 255a).

The Talmud (*Yoma* 38b) derives from this phrase that the world continues to exist even in the merit of one righteous person (צַדִּיק), because he is the *foundation of the world.*

Midrash Tanchuma (*Nitzavim* 2) elucidates this principle further, stating: "You are all guarantors for one another; even if there is [only] one righteous man among you, you all exist in his merit. Not only you [exist in his merit], but if there is one righteous man among you, the whole world exists in his merit, as it says, *And a righteous one is the foundation of the world.*"

The Vilna *Gaon,* commenting on these words, states that even after his death, a righteous person remains *the foundation of the world,* for his merit protects the world.

גִּלָּה מִדְרָשׁ הַנֶּעְלָם — *He revealed the "Hidden Midrash." Midrash HaNe-elam,* a mystical exposition on the commandments, authored by R' Shimon bar Yochai, is published as part of *Sefer HaZohar.*

יָכוֹל לִפְטוֹר הָעוֹלָם — *He could exonerate the world.* R' Shimon declared: "I am able to exempt the entire world from judgment from the day that I was born until now. And were my son, Elazar, with me, [we could exempt the world] from the day the world was created until now" (*Succah* 45b). See p. 75.

וְהִכְרִית אֶת הַקּוֹצִים — *And he cut away the thorns.* I.e., the wicked.

רָאָה פָנָיו מְאִירִים, בְּשִׁבְתּוֹ עִם חֲבֵרִים,
עֵת גִּלָּה סוֹד סְתָרִים, אֲדוֹנֵינוּ בַּר יוֹחָאי.
וַאֲמַרְתֶּם כֹּה לֶחָי, רַבִּי שִׁמְעוֹן בַּר יוֹחָאי,
וַאֲמַרְתֶּם כֹּה לֶחָי, אֲדוֹנֵינוּ בַּר יוֹחָאי.

He saw his face aglow when he sat with associates,
at the time when he revealed hidden secrets —
our master, Bar Yochai! *And you shall say . . .*

שָׁלוֹם רָב עַל מִשְׁכָּבוֹ, מַה יָּפְיוֹ וּמַה טּוּבוֹ,
דּוֹבֵר אֱמֶת בִּלְבָבוֹ, אֲדוֹנֵינוּ בַּר יוֹחָאי.
וַאֲמַרְתֶּם כֹּה לֶחָי, רַבִּי שִׁמְעוֹן בַּר יוֹחָאי,
וַאֲמַרְתֶּם כֹּה לֶחָי, אֲדוֹנֵינוּ בַּר יוֹחָאי.

Abundant peace upon his bier
How great is his beauty and his goodness,
he speaks truth in his heart —
our master, Bar Yochai! *And you shall say . . .*

תּוֹרָתוֹ מָגֵן לָנוּ, הִיא מְאִירַת עֵינֵינוּ,
הוּא יַמְלִיץ טוֹב בַּעֲדֵנוּ, אֲדוֹנֵינוּ בַּר יוֹחָאי.
וַאֲמַרְתֶּם כֹּה לֶחָי, רַבִּי שִׁמְעוֹן בַּר יוֹחָאי,
וַאֲמַרְתֶּם כֹּה לֶחָי, אֲדוֹנֵינוּ בַּר יוֹחָאי.

May his Torah shield us, it is the light of our eyes,
he will intercede for good on our behalf —
our master, Bar Yochai! *And you shall say . . .*

וְהִצִּיל הַלְּחוּצִים — *And rescued the oppressed.* The Talmud (*Me'ilah* 17a-b) relates that after the Destruction, the Romans issued a decree prohibiting observance of the Sabbath, circumcision and laws of family purity. The Sages decided to send R' Shimon "who is accustomed to miracles," to gain abolishment of the decree, and he succeeded.

בְּשִׁבְתּוֹ עִם חֲבֵרִים — *When he sat with associates.* With the חֲבְרַיָא קַדִּישָׁא, *Holy Fraternity,* the exalted group of disciples in whose presence R' Shimon revealed the Torah's secrets.

שָׁלוֹם רָב עַל מִשְׁכָּבוֹ — *Abundant peace upon his bier.* At the time of R' Shimon's interment, a Heavenly voice proclaimed, "He will come in peace, they will rest on their resting places" (from *Isaiah* 57:2).

R' Shimon's Praises — A Talmudic and Midrashic Selection

Sefer Shaarei Dimah offers the following selection of Talmudic and Midrashic passages which mention various qualities of R' Shimon bar Yochai. Their recitation is particularly auspicious for invoking R' Shimon's merit.

Mishnah Avos 4:17

רַבִּי שִׁמְעוֹן אוֹמֵר: שְׁלֹשָׁה כְתָרִים הֵן, כֶּתֶר תּוֹרָה וְכֶתֶר כְּהוּנָּה וְכֶתֶר מַלְכוּת, וְכֶתֶר שֵׁם טוֹב עוֹלֶה עַל גַּבֵּיהֶן:

Rabbi Shimon says: There are three crowns — the crown of Torah, the crown of priesthood, and the crown of kingship; but the crown of a good name surpasses them all.

Mishnah Avos 6:8

רַבִּי שִׁמְעוֹן בֶּן יְהוּדָה מִשּׁוּם רַבִּי שִׁמְעוֹן בֶּן יוֹחַאי אוֹמֵר: הַנּוֹי וְהַכֹּחַ וְהָעֹשֶׁר וְהַכָּבוֹד וְהַחָכְמָה וְהַזִּקְנָה וְהַשֵּׂיבָה וְהַבָּנִים, נָאֶה לַצַּדִּיקִים וְנָאֶה לָעוֹלָם, שֶׁנֶּאֱמַר, עֲטֶרֶת תִּפְאֶרֶת שֵׂיבָה בְּדֶרֶךְ צְדָקָה תִּמָּצֵא. וְאוֹמֵר, עֲטֶרֶת זְקֵנִים בְּנֵי בָנִים וְתִפְאֶרֶת בָּנִים אֲבוֹתָם. וְאוֹמֵר, תִּפְאֶרֶת בַּחוּרִים כֹּחָם וַהֲדַר זְקֵנִים שֵׂיבָה. וְאוֹמֵר, וְחָפְרָה הַלְּבָנָה וּבוֹשָׁה הַחַמָּה כִּי מָלַךְ ה' צְבָאוֹת בְּהַר צִיּוֹן וּבִירוּשָׁלַיִם וְנֶגֶד זְקֵנָיו כָּבוֹד.

Rabbi Shimon ben Yehudah says in the name of Rabbi Shimon ben Yochai: Beauty, strength, wealth, honor, wisdom, old age, hoary age and children —these befit the righteous and befit the world, as it is said: "Ripe old age is a crown of splendor, it can be found in the path of righteousness.[1]" And it says: "The crown of the aged is grandchildren, and the splendor of children is their fathers."[2] And it says: "The splendor of young men is their strength, and the

---

1. *Proverbs* 16:31.
2. Ibid. 17:6.

glory of old men is hoary age."[1] *And it says: "The moon will grow pale and the sun be shamed, when God, Master of Legions, will have reigned on Mount Zion and in Jerusalem, and honor shall be before his elders."*[2]

Shabbos 11a

תַּנְיָא, חֲבֵרִים שֶׁהָיוּ עוֹסְקִין בַּתּוֹרָה, מַפְסִיקִין לִקְרִיאַת שְׁמַע וְאֵין מַפְסִיקִין לִתְפִלָּה. אָמַר רַבִּי יוֹחָנָן: לֹא שָׁנוּ, אֶלָּא כְּגוֹן רַבִּי שִׁמְעוֹן בֶּן יוֹחַי וַחֲבֵרָיו שֶׁתּוֹרָתָן אוּמָנוּתָן. אֲבָל כְּגוֹן אָנוּ, מַפְסִיקִין לִקְרִיאַת שְׁמַע וְלִתְפִלָּה.

It was taught in a baraisa: Scholars who are studying Torah interrupt [their studies] for the recitation of Shema, but they do not interrupt [their studies] for prayer. R' Yochanan said: They taught [this ruling] only in regard to [people such as] R' Shimon bar Yochai and his colleagues whose sole occupation is their study of Torah. But people such as ourselves [who interrupt their studies for work], must interrupt their studies for the recitation of Shema and for prayer.

Gittin 67a

דְּתַנְיָא, אִיסִי בֶּן יְהוּדָה הָיָה מוֹנֶה שִׁבְחָן שֶׁל חֲכָמִים, רַבִּי מֵאִיר חָכָם וְסוֹפֵר. רַבִּי יְהוּדָה חָכָם לִכְשֶׁיִּרְצֶה. רַבִּי טַרְפוֹן גַּל שֶׁל אֱגוֹזִין. רַבִּי יִשְׁמָעֵאל חָנוּת מְיוּזֶּנֶת. רַבִּי עֲקִיבָא אוֹצָר בָּלוּם. רַבִּי

1. *Proverbs* 20:29.
2. *Isaiah* 24:23.

לִכְשֶׁיִּרְצֶה — *Whenever he chose.* He was able to immerse himself in his studies whenever he chose to do so, even when he was upset or troubled (*Maharitz Chayos*). See *Rashi* and *Maharsha.*

גַּל שֶׁל אֱגוֹזִין — *A pile of nuts.* When a nut is removed from the top of a pile, the remaining nuts fall on top of one another. Similarly, whenever a student questioned R' Tarfon, R' Tarfon answered the question and cited proofs from Scripture, *Midrash, Mishnah, Halachah* and *Aggadah* that supported his answer (*Avos D'Rav Nosson* quoted by *Rashi*).

חָנוּת מְיוּזֶּנֶת — *A wellstocked shop.* When a shop is wellstocked, the storekeeper

יוֹחָנָן בֶּן נוּרִי קוּפַּת הָרוֹכְלִים. רַבִּי אֶלְעָזָר בֶּן עֲזַרְיָה קוּפָּה שֶׁל בְּשָׂמִים. מִשְׁנַת רַבִּי אֱלִיעֶזֶר בֶּן יַעֲקֹב קַב וְנָקִי. רַבִּי יוֹסֵי נִמּוּקוֹ עִמּוֹ. רַבִּי שִׁמְעוֹן טוֹחֵן הַרְבֵּה וּמוֹצִיא קִימְעָא. תָּנָא, מְשַׁכֵּחַ קִימְעָא, וּמַה שֶּׁמּוֹצִיא אֵינוֹ מוֹצִיא אֶלָּא סוּבִּין. וְכֵן אָמַר רַבִּי שִׁמְעוֹן לְתַלְמִידָיו, בָּנַיי, שְׁנוּ מִדּוֹתַי, שֶׁמִּדּוֹתַי תְּרוּמוֹת מִתְּרוּמוֹת מִדּוֹתָיו שֶׁל רַבִּי עֲקִיבָא.

We learned in a baraisa: Isi ben Yehudah would enumerate the praiseworthy traits of various Sages: R' Meir was a scholar and a scribe. R' Yehudah was a scholar whenever he chose. R' Tarfon was like a pile of nuts. R' Yishmael was like a well-stocked shop. R' Akiva was like a storehouse with compartments. R' Yochanan ben Nuri was like a spice peddler's basket. R' Elazar ben Azariah was like a spice basket. The teachings of R' Eliezer ben Yaakov were

---

never keeps his customers waiting. Similarly, R' Yishmael was always prepared to teach [so that he never kept anyone waiting with an answer] (*Rashi*)].

אוֹצָר בָּלוּם — *A storehouse with compartments.* In his years as a student, Rabbi Akiva reviewed and recited his studies until he knew them proficiently. Later, when he became a great sage, he organized his knowledge according to subject and taught each subject separately (*Rashi*).

קוּפַּת הָרוֹכְלִים — *A spice peddler's basket.* Just as a spice peddler comes to town with a variety of spices, so did R' Yochanan ben Nuri have answers prepared for questions concerning Scripture, *Midrash, Halachah* and *Aggadah.* This praise is not as great as that accorded Rabbi Akiva, who initially studied many disciplines concurrently and only later organized his knowledge (*Rashi*).

קוּפָּה שֶׁל בְּשָׂמִים — *A spice basket.* This refers to a spice basket that one has at home which has less of a variety than that of a peddler. Also, a peddler wraps each spice individually to prepare it for customers (*Rashi*).

קַב וְנָקִי — *Measured but pure.* I.e, free of error. R' Eliezer taught less than his colleagues, but *halachah* is in accordance with all his teachings (*Rashi*)].

מַה שֶּׁמּוֹצִיא אֵינוֹ מוֹצִיא אֶלָּא סוּבִּין — *Whatever he releases is only bran.* Whatever R' Shimon bar Yochai may have forgotten were only rulings which were not in accordance with *halachah.*

תְּרוּמוֹת מִתְּרוּמוֹת — *The cream of the cream.* R' Shimon culled his teachings from the most select teachings of Rabbi Akiva; thus they went through two selection processes (*Rashi*).

measured but pure. R' Yose always has his reasons with him. R' Shimon grinds much but releases little.

We learned in a baraisa: He [R' Shimon] forgets little [of his learning] and whatever he releases is only bran. And this is what R' Shimon said to his students: "My sons, study my teachings, because my teachings are the cream of the cream of Rabbi Akiva's teachings."

Me'ilah 17a-17b

פַּעַם אַחַת גָּזְרָה מַלְכוּת גְּזֵרָה עַל יִשְׂרָאֵל, שֶׁלֹּא יִשְׁמְרוּ שַׁבָּת, וְשֶׁלֹּא יָמוּלוּ בְּנֵיהֶם, וְשֶׁיִּבְעֲלוּ נִדּוֹת. הָלַךְ רַבִּי רְאוּבֵן אִסְטַרְבּוּלִי וְסִפֵּר קוֹמִי וְהָלַךְ וְיָשַׁב עִמָּהֶם. אָמַר לָהֶם, מִי שֶׁיֵּשׁ לוֹ אוֹיֵב יַעֲנִי אוֹ יַעֲשִׁיר? אָמְרוּ לוֹ, יַעֲנִי. אָמַר לָהֶם, אִם כֵּן לֹא יַעֲשׂוּ מְלָאכָה בְּשַׁבָּת כְּדֵי שֶׁיַּעֲנוּ. אָמְרוּ טָבִיתָ, וּבִטְּלוּהָ. חָזַר וְאָמַר לָהֶן, מִי שֶׁיֵּשׁ לוֹ אוֹיֵב יַכְחִישׁ אוֹ יַבְרִיא? אָמְרוּ לוֹ, יַכְחִישׁ. אָמַר לָהֶם, אִם כֵּן יָמוּלוּ בְּנֵיהֶם לִשְׁמֹנָה יָמִים כְּדֵי שֶׁיַּכְחִישׁוּ. אָמְרוּ לוֹ, טָבִיתָ, וּבִטְּלוּהָ. חָזַר וְאָמַר לָהֶן, מִי שֶׁיֵּשׁ לוֹ אוֹיֵב יִרְבֶּה אוֹ יִתְמַעֵט? אָמְרוּ לוֹ, יִתְמַעֵט. אָמַר לָהֶם, אִם כֵּן לֹא יִבְעֲלוּ נִדּוֹת. אָמְרוּ טָבִיתָ, וּבִטְּלוּהָ. הִכִּירוּ בּוֹ שֶׁהוּא יְהוּדִי, הֶחֱזִירוּם. אָמְרוּ, מִי יֵלֵךְ וִיבַטֵּל אֶת הַגְּזֵרָה? יֵלֵךְ רַבִּי שִׁמְעוֹן בֶּן יוֹחַאי שֶׁהוּא מְלֻמָּד בַּנִּסִּים.

It happened once that the kingdom [of Rome] issued a decree against Israel that they should not observe the Sabbath, that they should not circumcise their sons and that they should not observe laws of family purity. Rabbi Reuven Istarboli went and cut his hair in a Roman style and sat among them [the Romans]. He said to them, "If one has an enemy, is it better that he should become poor or that he should become rich?" They reponded, "That he should become poor." He said to them, "If so, they should not work on the Sabbath so that they will become poor." They responded, "You are right," and annulled the decree.

He then said to them, "If someone has an enemy, is it better that he should become weakened or that he should become healthier?" They responded, "That he should become weakened." He said to them, "If so, their sons should be circumcised at eight days so that they will become weakened." They responded, "You are right," and annulled the decree.

He then said to them, "If one has an enemy, is it better that its population should increase or that it should decrease?" They responded, "That it should decrease." He said to them, "If so, they should not disregard the laws of family purity." They responded, "You are right," and annulled the decree.

But when they recognized that he [R' Reuven Istarboli] was a Jew, they reenacted the decrees. The Sages said, "Who shall go [now] and annul the decree? Let Rabbi Shimon ben Yochai go, for he is accustomed to miracles."

Yerushalmi Berachos 9:1

אָמַר רַבִּי חִזְקִיָּה בְּשֵׁם רַבִּי יִרְמְיָה, כָּל יָמָיו שֶׁל רַבִּי שִׁמְעוֹן בֶּן יוֹחַאי לֹא נִרְאֲתָה הַקֶּשֶׁת בֶּעָנָן.

Rabbi Chizkiyah said in the name of Rabbi Yirmiyah: All the days of Rabbi Shimon ben Yochai, the rainbow was not seen in a cloud.

Yerushalmi Shevi'is 9:1

רַבִּי שִׁמְעוֹן בֶּן יוֹחַאי הֲוָה עָבֵר בִּשְׁמִטְּתָא וְחָמֵי

מְלֻמָּד בְּנִסִּים — *Accustomed to miracles.* For miracles were done for him during his years in the cave (*Rashi*).

לֹא נִרְאֲתָה הַקֶּשֶׁת — *The rainbow was not seen.* See p. 104.

בִּשְׁמִטְּתָא — *During Shemittah.* The Torah dictates that every seventh year be observed as a Sabbatical year in the

חָד מְלַקֵּט שְׁבִיעִית. אֲמַר לֵיהּ, וְלַאו אָסוּר, וְלַאו סְפִיחִין אִנּוּן? אֲמַר לֵיהּ, וְלַאו אַנְתְּ מַתִּירָן? אֲמַר לֵיהּ, וְאֵין חֲבֵרַי חוֹלְקִין עָלַי? קָרָא עָלָיו, וּפוֹרֵץ גָּדֵר יִשְּׁכֶנּוּ נָחָשׁ. וְכֵן הֲוַת לֵיהּ.

Rabbi Shimon ben Yochai was walking during Shemittah and saw a person gathering Shemittah growths. He told the person, "Is this not forbidden? Are these not aftergrowths?" The person responded, "Are you not the one who permits them?" He [R' Shimon] retorted, "Do not my colleagues disagree with me?" He applied to him the verse, "And he who breaks down a wall will be bitten by a snake[1]*" — and that is what happened to him.*

Yerushalmi Sanhedrin 1:2

אָמַר רַבִּי עֲקִיבָא לְרַבִּי שִׁמְעוֹן בֶּן יוֹחַאי, דַּיֶּיךָ שֶׁאֲנִי וּבוֹרְאֲךָ מַכִּירִין עָרְכְּךָ.

Rabbi Akiva said to Rabbi Shimon ben Yochai: "It is sufficient that I and your Creator recognize your strength [i.e. your spiritual qualities]."

Bereishis Rabbah 35:2

רַבִּי חִזְקִיָּה בְּשֵׁם רַבִּי יִרְמְיָה אָמַר, כָּךְ אָמַר רַבִּי שִׁמְעוֹן בֶּן יוֹחַאי, בִּקְעָה בִּקְעָה אִמְּלַאי דִּינְרֵי זָהָב, וְנִתְמַלְּאָה.

1. *Ecclesiastes* 10:8.

Land of Israel. That year is known as *Shevi'is,* Seventh, or *Shemittah,* which literally means *relinquish* or *abandon* and reflects the relinquishing of control of one's agricultural produce and debts; see *Exodus* 23:11 and *Deuteronomy* 15:1-12.

סְפִיחִין — *Aftergrowths.* Aftergrowths are the new plants which sprout in a field from seeds which fell off the previous year's crops. Their status is the subject of a dispute between the Sages and R' Shimon in *Mishnah Shevi'is* 9:1.

אָמַר רַבִּי עֲקִיבָא — *Rabbi Akiva said*: see p. 43.

בִּקְעָה בִּקְעָה — *Valley Valley.* See p. 134.

Rabbi Chizkiah said in the name of Rabbi Yirmiyah: Rabbi Shimon bar Yochai said the following, "Valley, valley, become filled with dinarim of gold!" — and it became filled.

Bereishis Rabbah 35:2

רַבִּי חִזְקִיָּה בְּשֵׁם רַבִּי יִרְמְיָה אוֹמֵר, כַּךְ אָמַר רַבִּי שִׁמְעוֹן בֶּן יוֹחַאי, אִי בָּעֵי אַבְרָהָם לְמַקְרָבֵי מִן גַּבֵּהּ וְעַד גַּבִּי, וַאֲנָא מַקְרַב מִגַּבִּי עַד מַלְכָּא מְשִׁיחָא. וְאִן לָא בָעֵי, יִצְטָרֵף אֲחִיָּה הַשִּׁילוֹנִי עִמִּי, וַאֲנַן מַקְרְבִין מִן אַבְרָהָם עַד מַלְכָּא מְשִׁיחָא:

Rabbi Chizkiyah said in the name of Rabbi Yirmiyah: Rabbi Shimon bar Yochai said the following, "If Abraham wishes to bring near [the generations] from his day until mine [to the life of the World to Come], then I will bring near the generations from my day until the anointed king [Messiah]. And if not, then Achiyah the Shilonite will join me and we will bring near [the generations] from the days of Abraham until the anointed king."

אִי בָּעֵי אַבְרָהָם לְמִקְרְבֵי — *If Abraham wishes to bring near.* I.e., that he would bear the burden of the misdeeds of all the sinners of the world, and relieve them of the punishment due them in the World to Come (see *Rashi* to *Succah* 45b; see p. 75 in this volume).

אֲחִיָּה הַשִּׁילוֹנִי — *Achiyah the Shilonite.* See p. 174.

Upsherin (Chalakah) — The First Haircut

As discussed above, there is a widespread custom to cut a boy's hair for the first time on the Lag BaOmer closest to his third birthday. Below is a prayer from the days of the *Arizal* (1534-1572), to be recited upon cutting the child's hair.

יְהִי רָצוֹן מִלְּפָנֶיךָ, יהוה אֱלֹהֵי הָאֱלֹהִים וַאֲדוֹנֵי הָאֲדוֹנִים, שֶׁבִּזְכוּת כָּל הַצַּדִּיקִים וְהַחֲסִידִים מִיּוֹם שֶׁנִּבְרָא הָעוֹלָם וְעַד סוֹפוֹ, וּבִזְכוּת תּוֹרָתְךָ הַקְּדוֹשָׁה וְהַטְּהוֹרָה, וּבִזְכוּת מִצְוֹתֶיךָ וּשְׁמוֹתֶיךָ הַקְּדוֹשִׁים שֶׁבָּהּ, וּבִזְכוּת מִצְוַת פְּאַת הָרֹאשׁ שֶׁצִּוִּיתָנוּ בְּתוֹרָתֶיךָ: "לֹא תַקִּיפוּ פְּאַת רֹאשְׁכֶם", וּבִזְכוּת הַצַּדִּיק הַקָּדוֹשׁ הַזֶּה, מוֹרֵנוּ וְרַבֵּנוּ וַעֲטֶרֶת רֹאשֵׁנוּ, רַבִּי שִׁמְעוֹן בַּר יוֹחַאי כְּמוֹ שֶׁזָּכָה הַנַּעַר לִפְאַת הָרֹאשׁ, כֵּן יִזְכֶּה לְתוֹרָה וּלְחֻפָּה וּמִצְוֹת וּלְמַעֲשִׂים טוֹבִים, וְיוֹרֶה הוֹרָאוֹת בְּיִשְׂרָאֵל בְּחַיֵּי אָבִיו וּבְחַיֵּי אִמּוֹ, אָמֵן נֶצַח סֶלָה:

May it be Your will, Hashem, God of heavenly forces and Master of masters, that in the merit of all the righteous and exceedingly pious from the day the world was created until its end, in the merit of Your holy and pure Torah, in the merit of Your holy commandments and Names contained within it, in the merit of the commandment of "the peyos (corners) of the head" regarding which You commanded us in Your Torah, "You shall not round off the edge of your scalp,"[1] and in the merit of this holy righteous one, our guide and teacher, the crown of our head Rabbi Shimon bar Yochai: Just as this youth merited peyos of the head, so should he merit [to enter into] the Torah, the wedding canopy, commandments and to good deeds; and may he merit to teach [Torah] laws in Israel in the lifetime of his father and in the lifetime of his mother. Amen, eternally, forever.

The following psalm is then recited:

הַלְלוּיָהּ, הַלְלוּ אֵל בְּקָדְשׁוֹ, הַלְלוּהוּ בִּרְקִיעַ עֻזּוֹ. הַלְלוּהוּ בִגְבוּרֹתָיו, הַלְלוּהוּ כְּרֹב גֻּדְלוֹ. הַלְלוּהוּ בְּתֵקַע שׁוֹפָר, הַלְלוּהוּ בְּנֵבֶל וְכִנּוֹר. הַלְלוּהוּ בְתֹף וּמָחוֹל, הַלְלוּהוּ בְּמִנִּים וְעֻגָב. הַלְלוּהוּ בְצִלְצְלֵי שָׁמַע, הַלְלוּהוּ בְּצִלְצְלֵי תְרוּעָה. כֹּל הַנְּשָׁמָה תְּהַלֵּל יָהּ הַלְלוּיָהּ:

Halleluyah! Praise God in His Sanctuary; praise Him in the firmament of His power. Praise Him for His mighty acts; praise Him as befits His abundant greatness. Praise Him with the blast of the shofar; praise Him with lyre and harp. Praise Him with drum and dance; praise Him with organ and flute. Praise him with clanging cymbals; praise Him with resonant trumpets. Let all souls praise God, Halleluyah!

Prayer of the Chazon Ish

The following prayer, composed by R' Avraham Yeshayahu Karelitz, author of *Chazon Ish,*[1] can be recited by parents in the daily *Shemoneh Esrei* in the blessing of שְׁמַע קוֹלֵנוּ (before the words כִּי אַתָּה שׁוֹמֵעַ ...); at the conclusion of *Shemoneh Esrei* at the close of אֱלֹקַי נְצֹר; and at other times. Surely it is appropriate for the day of a child's *upsherin.*

יְהִי רָצוֹן מִלְּפָנֶיךָ יהוה אֱלֹהֵינוּ וֵאלֹהֵי אֲבוֹתֵינוּ, שֶׁתְּרַחֵם עַל־בְּנִי (שֵׁם הַבֵּן) בֶּן (שֵׁם הָאֵם) וְתַהֲפוֹךְ אֶת־לְבָבוֹ לְאַהֲבָה וּלְיִרְאָה שְׁמֶךָ וְלִשְׁקוֹד בְּתוֹרָתְךָ הַקְּדוֹשָׁה וְתָסִיר מִלְּפָנָיו כָּל־הַסִּיבּוֹת הַמּוֹנְעוֹת אוֹתוֹ מִשְּׁקִידַת תּוֹרָתְךָ הַקְּדוֹשָׁה, וְתָכִין אֶת כָּל־הַסִּיבּוֹת הַמְּבִיאוֹת לְתוֹרָתְךָ הַקְּדוֹשָׁה:

May it be Your will, Hashem, our God and the God of our forefathers, that You have mercy on my son [son's Hebrew name] *son of* [mother's Hebrew name], *and direct his heart to love and fear Your Name, and to be diligent in the study of Your holy Torah. May You remove from before him all circumstances that may deter him from diligent study of Your holy Torah and may You make ready all the conditions that will bring him [closer] to Your holy Torah.*

---

1. It is found in *Kovetz Igros Chazon Ish,* I, §74. The Chazon Ish would say that prayers of parents on behalf of their children are particularly potent. See *Sforno* to *Genesis* 31:1.

This volume is part of
THE ARTSCROLL SERIES®
an ongoing project of
translations, commentaries and expositions
on Scripture, Mishnah, Talmud, Halachah,
liturgy, history and the classic Rabbinic writings;
and biographies, and thought.

For a brochure of current publications
visit your local Hebrew bookseller
or contact the publisher:

Mesorah Publications, ltd

4401 Second Avenue
Brooklyn, New York 11232
(718) 921-9000